INTRODUCTION TO THE
PHILOSOPHY OF RELIGION

Introduction to the Philosophy of Religion

BY

James F. Ross

THE MACMILLAN COMPANY
COLLIER-MACMILLAN LTD., LONDON

TO SEAMUS, ELLEN-MARIE, RICHARD-FALLON
AND THERESE

Library of Congress Catalog Card Number: 74–80298

FIRST PRINTING

The Macmillan Company
Collier-Macmillan Canada Ltd., Toronto, Ontario

Printed in the United States of America

Some of the material in this book is from *Philosophical Theology* by James F. Ross, copyright © 1969 by The Bobbs-
Merrill Company, Inc., and is reprinted by permission of the
publisher.

Contents

Introduction

WHAT IS PHILOSOPHY OF RELIGION? It is the philosophical examination of religion: the methodical, critical assessment of religious belief, experience, and worship and of the theological concepts, arguments, and systems which have been thought to provide an abstract and coherent explanation of religious belief, experience, and worship.

We can no more easily say what religion is than we can what philosophy is. In fact, part of the task for the philosopher is to formulate an acceptable and generally applicable concept of religion.

Although there is not agreement among philosophers on how theoretically to characterize religion, still, since it is widely agreed that Christianity and Buddhism and Judaism, etc., are definitely and paradigmatically religions, the philosophical investigation of particular religions can proceed, leaving the analysis of the concept "religion" to be undertaken in its proper and separate place.

In general terms, the philosopher approaches a certain class of religious beliefs and phenomena, say those of Christianity or Judaism or the combined tradition (as we shall do), and he asks: (a) Under what criteria are those beliefs meaningful? (b) Are they true? How can one discover or come to know this? (c) What values do such beliefs confer upon individuals; what functions do they serve? (d) How do the believers know (in a nontheoretical way) that their beliefs are true (not, why do they say so)? (e) What kinds of things must there be in the universe if these religious beliefs are true? And so on.

The philosopher looks at the religious belief and the religious believers from his vantage as epistemologist (who wonders what sort of thing a "person" must be if persons do this or that, etc.; and what "knowing" is, if we are to countenance knowledge); as a theorist of value (who wonders what function or value is served by the belief, the experiences, the practices); as a metaphysician (what *is* there in the universe); as a moral theorist (what courses of action would be right and what concepts of "good," "right," and "ought" are fitting to the person who believes thus and so). So one can say that philosophy of religion is the epistemological, ethical, psychological, metaphysical, and logical investigation into the nature, grounds, and functions of religious faith (usually as manifested in a particular religion). It is entirely a theoretical enterprise, with no concern for the conversion of anyone.

This means that at various times we shall encounter questions which in order to be answered require that we should have at hand a reply to some general epistemological, metaphysical, logical, psychological, or moral puzzle (of which our religious question is only a single instance). It means that philosophy of religion is a piggyback science in which the body of religious belief is placed on the backs of five philosophical horses (epistemology, psychology, metaphysics, ethics, and logic) which ride off each in its own direction and into the midst of its own herd of problems. We then observe how well the body of religious belief will stretch, and, when the strain finally comes, we watch carefully to see whether it is due to weakness of the horse (the particular, partially developed general science) or to the weakness of the rider (the religious faith).

We can recognize a religion at least some of the times that we confront one. And we can see the Judaic-Christian tradition of beliefs about the existence, nature, action, and purposes of God and its corresponding beliefs about the nature, obligations, origin and destiny of man, as the religion most closely associated with our Western culture. This is not to suggest that any other religion, Buddhism, Confucianism, etc., would be theoretically of less interest to investigate; nor is it to suggest that expressed beliefs are indubitably central to religion. But the students should know that he cannot productively investigate what he does not, to a significant extent, already understand. And Westerners, on the whole, know very little of the content of Eastern religion. We shall therefore confine our attention in this introduction entirely to the context of the central religious trend in Western culture: the Judaic-Christian tradition.

METHOD

There are as many ways of doing philosophy of religion as there are ways of doing philosophy and they are many indeed, ranging from highly formalistic and mathematized approaches, through the loose, aphoristic, and prophetic forms which border on poetry (and sometimes nonsense.). Naturally, we shall in this introduction avoid the more extreme techniques (not, however, denying that they have been followed by some thinkers of distinction). Still, we must choose among three current and respected methods of philosophy: the analytic, the existential, and the phenomenological.

Nor can we elect our method by claiming that it alone among its contemporaries is the perennial method of Western philosophy. Practitioners of all three methods claim that and claim further that their methods are especially fitted for the philosophy of religion. Therefore, without prejudice to the fact that existential philosophy is especially suited for the inquiry of those who are desperately and intimately concerned with the search for a way of life, and without ignoring the resources of phenomenological analysis for disclosing and unraveling those basic ideas which over and over occur in our discussions, we shall follow primarily the analytical method, one of abstract but rigorous argument which is mainly characteristic of philosophy in America and Britain, recommending the method only in terms of the results we shall display through its application. A more sophisticated comparison of the advantages of differing methods in the area of philosophy of religion is inappropriate to a general introduction and would only delay our coming to grips with the central problems.

THE PROBLEMS

There are more philosophical problems connected with religion than we can usefully mention. Just consider the supposedly simple question: What is religion? Or the questions: What is religious faith? What is divine goodness? What is omnipotence? Could God reveal Himself in such a way that no rational creature could fail to recognize Him? Can we show the human person to be immortal? By what features could you recognize a vision of God if you had one? What are miracles and how could one recognize one?

About each of these, and thousands more, discussion could be virtually endless. So, too, we could generate an endless peripheral discussion if we pretended that the problems which we shall consider in detail are the most important or the most fundamental ones. Therefore, let us be content with this: The problems we consider are: (1) among those to which the great philosophers have directed explicit attention, (2) among those which are surrounded by very interesting arguments, and (3) among those to which recent philosophers have made worthy contributions.

For the understanding of this introduction to the subject it is crucial that the student recognize the fundamental difference between the first two chapters. One is concerned with the philosophical establishment of the existence of God and the theoretical definition of the attributes and nature of God; the other, with a philosophical critique of nontheoretical knowledge of God. In the first we are interested in attempts by philosophers and theologians to establish that God exists and that God has certain attributes. In the second we are interested in philosophical explanations of how religious believers could have knowledge (or, at least, justified belief) through their religion, belief which they have, in the main, acquired through religious instruction but without benefit of theoretical and systematic investigations.

Even if one could conclude that we cannot establish the existence of God or that God has certain attributes (e.g., that He "created the visible world"), this would still leave open the question of whether religious believers have knowledge of God's existence or His nature or are justified in believing in God, in believing that God exists, that God has a certain nature, and that God has certain purposes to work out in the universe. For it should be most obvious, even to a beginner in philosophy, that if religious believers (on the whole) do have justified belief in these things, it is not through any philosophical or theoretical argument they possess; most people have never heard of the arguments we shall discuss and would only distort them or find them superfluous if they encountered them. Whatever the justification the believer may have, it's something which is his own and is not something to be provided by the speculations of the metaphysician. A *theoretical* consideration of whether believers are or could be justified in their religious beliefs is the subject of the second chapter.

In the third chapter we discuss the topic of evil (with some animadversions to determinism and predestination). The subject has always functioned centrally in philosophical and theological inquiry and has been intensively debated in our century with what I take to be notable advances.

It is of great value to the student to recognize that unresolved problems of logic, of theory of knowledge, ethics and metaphysics recur full-grown in other areas of philosophy and demand our recourse to the general epistemological, ethical, and metaphysical contexts where they are treated with a family of similar questions. The problem of evil is an especially good example of such a recurrence of problems belonging to other areas of philosophy —particularly ethics, metaphysics, and logic.

The fourth chapter consists of an introduction to the theory of analogy which is the "classical" systematic answer to the question as to whether religious discourse is cognitively meaningful. Combining Chapter Four, which is a portion of a general theory of meaning, with Chapter Two, which is a partial account of the origins of nontheoretical knowledge of God, we have an affirmative alternative to the attacks upon the possibility of religious knowledge which are based upon the "verifiability" and related criteria of meaning and which conclude that religious knowledge is impossible because the discourse in which the religion is expressed is without intelligible content. It is the assumption of this chapter that the recent disputes over cognitive meaningfulness of religious discourse have largely missed the point, and that a more fruitful discussion of "religious knowledge" should be founded upon: (a) a reconstruction of the theory of analogy; (b) an examination of the nature of testimonial evidence; (c) an examination of religous experience as an instance of perceptual knowledge.

Finally, it may be of use to list here some of the characteristic claims which are argued or urged in this introduction:

(a) "Proofs" or establishment of the existence of God are part of a theoretical enterprise and have their value as good or bad arguments independently of whether they are convincing to anyone. Such theoretical proofs are disengaged from the acquisition or abandonment of religious belief.

(b) There appear to be some theoretical arguments for the existence of God which make perfectly reasonable assumptions, are logically consistent in form, and lead to the conclusion that a being capable of divinity exists necessarily.

(c) Theoretical considerations suggest that the principle of sufficient reason is false, that God is not the sufficient reason for the world (in the way classical theologians thought), and that God "accounts" for the world by being the logically necessary condition for the *possibility* that the world is explained or accounted for.

(d) Religious knowledge can indeed be transmitted by a chain of testimony which originates in the experiences of apostles and prophets.

(e) There is nothing about the supposed originating experiences of apostles and prophets that displays an epistemological deficit on their part which is not shared by human experience in general; as a result, one cannot *a priori* deny the possibility that religious knowledge came to mankind in that way.

(f) With due attention to the way perceptual sets and significance-assignments affect human experience, there is no *theoretical* reason why the apostles and prophets did not know by experience exactly what they pretended to know.

(g) There is no reason to believe on the basis of what we know about the relationship of God and the world that God is *not* good or is limited in power because of the evils in the world. In fact, we can see that all such forms of reasoning will be logically mistaken or epistemologically circular.

(h) There is no reason to believe religious discourse to be cognitively meaningless; there is every reason to believe that an adequate theory of language can be constructed which will display the *cognitive continuity* of discourse in religious and nonreligious contexts.

CHAPTER I

Philosophical Establishment of the Existence and Nature of God

INITIAL CONSIDERATIONS

What Sort of Being Do We Inquire About?

IF YOU THINK that just because we have restricted our discussions to the context of the Judaic-Christian tradition, we can simply say what are the characteristics a thing must have to be God, you are mistaken. It is not obvious from the Holy Scriptures that it is an essential or defining characteristic of God that He knows everything (including the sum of two arbitrarily chosen imaginary numbers); nor is it obvious from Scripture and tradition that God is omnipresent or that God has no accidental or acquired characteristics. We must, unfortunately, select a subtradition which we consider to embody the "orthodox" or "proper" description of God.

We shall do so, without further preface: God is a being which is infinite (unlimited by any other, whether actual or possible), omnipotent, eternal, omnipresent, omniscient, a disembodied intelligence, benevolent, morally perfect, aesthetically admirable, worthy of worship, and personal (in the sense that He can enter into encounter and communication with the finite persons He has created).

Some students object to our beginning with a "definition of God," saying that a definition prejudices inquiry, especially when they are told that *whether* the being exists is a dependent function of *what sort of* a being it is (as is argued by Anselm and Descartes). This is both right and wrong. Certainly some restrictions on the term "God" are appropriate. After all, if "God" meant "the 1966 Volkswagen," it would be an easy and empirical matter to prove the existence of such a being. We would need only to go to the dealer's showroom. Moreover, a person who meant that by the term "God" would be childish. But what of the person who means "a being which is finite in power and knowledge but is creator of the world, etc."? There is nothing wrong with his definition of the term "God," as such. We can criticize the definitions of such a term only in some determined context of correct use. Where ordinary contexts are many, diverse, inconsistent, and vague we have to seek additional restrictions from contexts which we consider "authoritative" in some sense. Hence we turn to a class of theologians whom we consider to be *orthodox* on the point and fill out our concepts with theirs. Should someone wish to alter or eliminate various characteristics, that is his privilege. As long as you are clear about what sort of being it is whose existence or nonexistence you wish to establish, you have complete freedom to frame your definition as you wish. But if you want to know whether there is any such being as the Christians and the Jews think exists and is to be called "God," you must frame your definition in a way which will make your answer relevant to their beliefs. If you wonder why we need any definition at all, you should now know that we need it in order to know what we are talking about, in order to know what claims and criticisms are relevant to our inquiry. With no description or definition to work from, we will literally fail to know what we are talking about.

But our characterization of God is neither religiously nor theologically neutral: it is not common to several religions and further involves certain ideas like "morally perfect" and "omniscient" which are apparently inexplicable apart from philosophical or theological theory developed by religious systematizers. Is that bad? Since we restrict ourselves to the Judaic-Christian tradition, there is no defect in our not using a minimal concept "God" which would be applicable to all religions and to all things people call "God"; why, there may be no concept "God" which will be adequate for all religions! (Try to formulate one.) The fact that our description contains some system-bound concepts (morally perfect, omniscient, eternal) is a limitation but not a defect, provided we later explain these ideas without having to accept the whole system of philosophical thought from which they arose. I think the reduction of these system-bound concepts to unbound concepts can be made in its appropriate place. So, though we admit that the characteristics which are made essential to God are themselves in need of explanation, this is not a defect in the enterprise of describing God. We have to get off the ground sometime and can unwrap our baggage later.

We must explicitly admit that the concept "God" we employ is one representative of the Judaic-Christian tradition, but that it is not equally representative of all strands of that tradition; and, further, that the characteristic attributes we associate with the term "God" are themselves in need of philosophical explanation and interrelation.

What Must We Require of Arguments to Show That There is Such a Being?

For many centuries there has been confusion about the function of arguments for the existence of God. Some writers like St. Anselm appear to have thought their arguments were sufficient to convince anyone who understood them. Others may have thought their arguments were primarily useful for the conversion of unbelievers and for the strengthening of the faith of the reader. A few writers seem to have thought that arguments for the existence of God are chiefly useful as parts of philosophical and theological theory with little relevance to practical faith. The student must not take these alternatives as if they were *clearly* envisioned by the classical philosophers as objectives among which they might choose; the orientation of a particular author was often determined by the circumstances under which he did his work rather than by conscious selection.

Some Facts

Very few persons who believe there is a god of the sort supposed by the Judaic-Christian tradition have come to this belief by any formal process of reasoning or argumentation; by far the largest percentage of believers have acquired their faith through the *teaching* (not the reasoning or argumentation) of parents, pastors and their cultural environment. If such believers really do have knowledge of or justified belief in the existence of God, it is obvious that it was not acquired through arguments for the existence of God. Among the relatively small group of persons who come to believe that there is a god of the sort supposed by the Judaic-Christian tradition and who become religious believers as adults through the process of conversion, there are still very few who reached their beliefs through arguments; but there are a significant number whose beliefs have been buttressed and perhaps even precipitated through popularizations of the "design" and "first cause" arguments. That these popularized versions have neither the merit of validity nor that of true premises is incidental to the midwifery they provide for the nascent faith of the convert-to-be. People, on the whole, are simply not converted through arguments nor are their children, born in the faith, initially educated through arguments.

Arguments for the existence of God, if they have any value at all in the formation of religious faith, have that value tangentially to some other purpose they serve.

A Question of Purpose

From what we know now about human psychology we can see how pointless it would be for a philosopher to think that he could frame an argument which will convince everyone who understands it. Some people are so profoundly prejudiced that, although they see what you are saying, they cannot see that what you are saying is true, even if it is. This holds not only for religion but for politics, morality, art, practical affairs and every area of human action wherein a man's desires can become the ruler of his intellect. Hence, it is childish to think you can convince everyone who understands you by means of one informal (or formal) argument; there are some people who would fail to be convinced no matter what argument you gave them. Therefore, St. Anselm was just wrong and plainly in ignorance of human folly when he thought that his argument would convince everyone, even the Psalmist's fool "who says in his heart 'there is no God.'" If you expect the philosopher to produce an argument which will or could convince everyone who understands it, you are asking more than any human can do. It is no just criticism to say that a philosopher has failed to convince you; that may tell us more about you than it does about his work.

It is equally hopeless to think you can begin an argument from facts which are obvious to *everyone*; there is no reason to think that there is very much or even anything which everyone knows. *A fortiori* there is no reason to think everyone knows what is needed as the starting point for an "effective" argument for the existence of God.

But what would an "effective" argument for the existence of God be like? If it does not have to convince (in the sense of "bring x to know") everyone, if it does not have to begin from premises which everyone knows, what does it have to be like?

There are certain minimal conditions which no one could reasonably dispute. (1) An effective argument must have true premises and a true conclusion. It would surely be worthless if it began with what is false or if it began with the truth and concluded with what is false. (2) An effective argument must be logically valid; it must not be possible to construct a parallel argument which will begin with true premises and end in a false conclusion. Combining the first two properties, truth of premises and validity of form, we define the property "soundness" which is the first and indispensable requirement of an effective argument. A sound argument can be constructed for any true proposition.

To remind you of this fact. Consider any two true propositions, p and q. We can always construct the following two sound arguments:

(a) 1. $p \supset q$ (b) 4. $q \supset p$

      2. p 5. q

      3. q 6. p

Any two true propositions are "materially" equivalent and thus materially imply one another, with the result that lines 1 and 4 must be true if both p and q are true. But lines 2 and 5 are true by the suppositions of the case we consider, and are sufficient, therefore, to render 1 and 4 true. Hence all our premises are true, as well as our conclusions. But the form of our argument is *modus ponens* (an inference from the truth of the antecedent to the truth of the consequent) the key elementary valid argument form. Hence, both arguments are valid and have true premises; therefore, they are sound. Since p and q stand for any two true propositions, it follows that we can construct a sound argument for any true proposition. Since by trivial manipulations we can create an infinite number of true propositions from two true propositions, we can get an infinite number of true premises for any true conclusion. Hence, no one can consistently believe that God exists and that no sound argument for this conclusion can be constructed. So much the worse for certain theologians who thought so.

Yet, soundness of argument alone will not fulfill the purposes of arguments for the existence of God.

But this brings us back to our key question. What purpose is an argument (of the sort designed by the classical philosophers who wrote about the existence of God) supposed to serve? We have already eliminated the objectives of convincing everyone, most people, or even a large number of people on the ground that people do not normally acquire beliefs about such all-important matters as the existence of God by means of formal arguments. We have also eliminated the objective of beginning with "what everyone knows" on the ground that there is no such body of knowledge held in common by everyone. We have, in effect, eliminated religious purposes as the primary function to be served by arguments for the existence of God; this is not at all to deny that such arguments may serve to support, or even to precipitate the religious faith of some or even many persons; it is merely to insist that whether or not an argument will serve those functions is incidental and inessential to its intrinsic merits. The purpose to be served by the traditional arguments for the existence of God is philosophical: the arguments are supposed to provide a *theoretical establishment* of the conclusion that God exists.

What is a Theoretical Establishment?

It is a proof according to the standards of correct abstract thought. The premises have to be publicly testable by means of a philosophical investigation and must have their truth or falsity decidable, at least in principle, through the application of thought according to the methods of the philosopher. The structure of the argument has to be such that one could come to see that its premises are true without already having as grounds for this knowledge, one's knowledge that the conclusion is true—it must not be circular. While there is not widespread agreement over what is involved in "being publicly testable by means of a philosophical investigation," it is already evident that we simply must not ask of a philosophical argument that it should convince anyone in particular or even, perhaps, anyone at all. The whole point of such arguments is quite different from that of bringing individual people to know what they did not know before.

The arguments for the existence of God which are examined by the philosopher are much more like the arguments for some hypothesis in physics or some other pure science than they are like the arguments between football buffs over which strategy a coach should adopt. Whether they are good, effective arguments or not is to be decided through investigation according to the methods of the appropriate abstract science and is to be decided without consideration of the personal convictions or conversion of any individual.

The classical arguments are in no wise weakened or properly criticized merely by your saying that they do not satisfy you. You must enter into the context of purely theoretical criticism and present objections based upon reasons and plausible arguments, just as you would have to do in criticizing an argument by Euclid or Einstein in their respective fields of inquiry. (Can you imagine that Pythagoras should feel justly criticized because you find his demonstration of his key theorem to be unconvincing?)

It is because of this most important distinction between the proper context in which to view the classical arguments for the existence of God and the proper context in which to criticize the process by which individual religious believers acquire their beliefs (which is little or not at all through the classical arguments for the existence of God), that I have made such a clear demarcation between the first two chapters. First we are concerned with arguments presented in the context of abstract systematic philosophy (regardless of what confusion there may be about the uses to which the arguments were originally to be put). Then in the second chapter we consider the nontheoretical knowledge of God which is claimed by many religious persons and undertake a philosophical examination of the nature and ground for such knowledge. That chapter is primarily an application of the general study of theory of knowledge to the particular context of knowledge of "religious" truths. In that section we shall explain how the philosophical arguments discussed in the first chapter may serve important tangential and incidental purposes in the creation of knowledge of God among those who pursue such knowledge as existentially concerned human beings. Whether the philosophical arguments we are about to discuss succeed or fail in serving these purposes is wholly inconsequential to their inherent merits and defects, which will be explained in the following pages.

We can go even further, saying that whether or not a given argument for the existence of God (or, for that matter, an argument for any philosophical conclusion whatever) fails to convince everyone, everyone who understands it, some people or even anyone at all is entirely incidental to what may be its true merit. For, it is conceivable that philosophers should produce a perfectly sound argument which is not circular and with premises whose truth is definitely discoverable through philosophical investigation, and yet whose premises are such that no one knows enough (other than perhaps the author) to see that they are true. It fails to convince anyone at all, but it still has the intrinsic structure sufficient to create knowledge of its conclusion for a person who knows enough to see that it is sound. So, a good argument need actually convince no one.

Paradoxical? Yes. But you will best grasp the whole question by defending one of the opposed views, by insisting that an argument for the existence of God (and for any other philosophical conclusion) must convince everyone who understands it, or convince someone who understands it. How will you decide whom it must convince? And under what circumstances must it convince such persons? Can you construct a sound argument which is not circular and will fail to convince someone who understands it? If you try these things diligently, you may still dislike the conclusion I suggest, but you will understand what is problematical about the requirements which an argument must satisfy and how careful you must be if you wish to be fair to the whole enterprise of arguing for or against the existence of God or some other philosophical conclusion.

Our question was: what must we require of arguments to show that there is such a being? We can answer as follows: such arguments must be sound; they must be noncircular; they must have premises which are publicly testable (and not only through some inner and unrepeatable experience); their premises must be, at least in principle, decidable through a philosophical examination.

The nature of a "philosophical examination" and the ways it will differ from simple experimental verification still need to be explained. But the student does best to leave such points open until he sees how such criticism is actually conducted. The best way to learn philosophical method is not to hear it described, but to enter its spirit as it is applied.

Distinguishing Some Questions

When some people read St. Anselm's argument to show that there is something which exists and which is such that nothing more perfect is conceivable, or St. Thomas Aquinas' argument to show that there exists a first uncaused cause, or the argument to show that there exists an intelligent designer of the universe, they say, "Even if we granted that the argument is sound, it would not prove God exists because it only proves that some first cause, intelligent designer or most perfect conceivable being exists." And they take this to be a decisive objection because the author of the argument has not shown (by another argument?) that this being is God. However, to look at the arguments this way is to distort the historical context in which they originated. They were part of a process of establishing the existence of God and are only the first or existential step: to show that the being, which God is, exists. It is entirely a separate matter to show that the being whose existence is established is *identical* with God. The reasoning by which the existent is identified as having all the essential attributes of God is not part of the existence-argument itself but must be sought outside it. Hence, "Does God exist?" is a complex question. One can think of answers in the form of an argument to show that a certain sort of being exists, without asking for a separate and detailed identification in it of all the characteristics of God which we listed earlier, and one can demand the completion of the whole systematic enterprise of establishing both the existence and the identification. If one demands the latter, it is unfair to tax the initial arguments for not supplying it. If one wants only the former, then to say the authors have failed to establish the existence of God requires that one show where the argument is defective, or show that such a being could not be identified with God. It is unfair to criticize an argument for failing to achieve what it never set out to do.

THE PHILOSOPHICAL ARGUMENTS

A great many philosophers have offered arguments to show that some being which can be identified as God exists. In fact, there are so many different arguments that there is a variety of ways to classify them, a variety rendered bewildering because essentially the same argument has often been treated as being of quite diverse sorts. In an introduction to the philosophy of religion it is usual to concentrate upon the classical prototypes—the arguments of St. Anselm, those of St. Thomas and the so-called moral arguments. Our only innovations will be to discuss Spinoza's argument based upon the Principle of Sufficient Reason and to mention another type which originates with the Arabian medievals and with Duns Scotus—the Modal Argument.

St. Anselm (1033-1109): *The Ontological Argument*[1]

Even a fool can understand that God is "a being than which nothing greater can be conceived," begins the great medieval theologian. Such a being "exists in the understanding," as is obvious since we think of it. Either it exists only as thought of or it exists in reality as well. Suppose it exists only as thought of; then we can think of something which is in every respect the same except that *it* exists in reality as well as in thought; this latter thing would be better than the former since it surpasses the former in having real existence as well as existence as-something-thought-of. However, the former cannot then be something than which a greater cannot be conceived (for we just conceived a greater). Therefore, only a being which exists in *reality* as well as in thought can be such that nothing greater *can be conceived*: so, that-than-which-nothing-greater-can-be-conceived really exists.

[1] The name "ontological argument" was given to Anselm's reasoning by Immanuel Kant in his immortal discussion of its soundness. See *St. Anselm's Basic Writings: Proslogiom, Monologiom, Cur Deus Homo*, 2d ed., translated by S. W. Deane (Lasalle, Illinois, Open Court Publishing Co., 1962).

In Anselm's words: "If that-than-which-a-greater cannot-be-thought is in the understanding alone, this same thing, than-which-a-greater-*cannot*-be-thought, is also that-than-which-a-greater-*can*-be-thought. But this is clearly impossible. Doubtless, then, there exists both in the understanding and in reality a being-than-which-a-greater-cannot-be-thought."

Naturally, St. Anselm does not mean "greater" in any physical sense; he means it in an evaluative sense: "more perfect," "more excellent," or "more worthy of admiration." And, as is evident in the paraphrase which precedes his words, "to exist in the understanding" means merely to exist as something which is thought of. It is perfectly correct for one to say "there *is* something which I am thinking of—a purple unicorn." Thus the heart of Anselm's first argument is that if the being we are thinking of when we think of what is such that nothing more perfect can be conceived does *not* really exist, then we cannot have been consistent in our thought—because a being which is really existent and was in every other respect the same would be more perfect. The only thing we can be thinking of, if we think consistently, when we think of a being than which nothing more perfect is conceivable is a really existing being. We cannot be thinking of a really existing being unless such a being actually exists.

Let us consider a second (among several others) version in which Anselm's reasoning appears in the *Proslogiom* and in his reply to the objections of the Monk Gaunilo.

Everything which can exist falls into one of two classes: those things which *can* be thought of as not-existing and those things which *cannot* be thought of as not-existing. Whatever can exist and cannot be thought of as not-existing must be more perfect than any member of the first class. Now if that than which nothing greater can be conceived does not fall into the second class (the things which cannot be thought of as not-existing) then such a being cannot be that-than-which-nothing-greater-can-be-conceived, because *every* member of the second class (because of the fact that it can exist and cannot be thought not-to-exist) will be something more perfect than it. Hence, that-than-which-nothing-greater-can-be-conceived must be such that it cannot (consistently) be *thought* not-to-exist. Whatever cannot (consistently) be thought not-to-exist must, of necessity, exist. Therefore that-than-which-nothing-greater-can-be-conceived exists necessarily.[2]

Comments: The great fertility of these arguments is indicated first by the fact that most great philosophers from Aquinas, Scotus, and Bonaventure through Descartes, Spinoza, and Immanuel Kant have felt compelled to take a position for or against them. Secondly, discussion of these arguments has flourished in the last thirty years, with the greater number of papers appearing in the last decade.[3]

---

[2] St. Anselm puts the point this way: ". . . Something can be thought of as existing which cannot be thought of as not existing, and this is greater than that which *can* be thought of as not existing. So, if that, than which a greater cannot be thought, can be thought of as not existing, this very thing than which a greater cannot be thought is *not* that than which a greater cannot be thought. But that is contradictory. Therefore, there truly exists a being than which a greater cannot be thought—so truly that it cannot even be thought of as not existing."

[3] Charles Hartshorne has argued effectively that the real merits of the argument have eluded most critics. See *Man's Vision of God* (New York, Harper & Row, Inc., 1941); *The Logic of Perfection* (Lasalle, Illinois, Open Court Publishing Co., 1962); and his introduction to the Open Court Anselm Selections (Note 1 above). Norman Malcolm, in "Anselm's Ontological Arguments," *Philosophical Review* (January

Thirdly, it is one of the more humorous features of the history of philosophy that while the predominant reaction to Anselm's reasoning is to pronounce it fatally ill, no two prognosticators seem to agree on just what is wrong with it or even upon which of its elements are symptomatic of its defects. Fourthly, and most importantly, the questions which have been opened by this argument and the inquiries it has occasioned have been impressive indeed—e.g., whether "existence" is a predicate; whether it is legitimate to argue from the nature of what must be thought about reality to the nature of reality irrespective of our thought; whether something can exist necessarily; whether an existential conclusion can be derived from necessary premises.

The first important objector, a monk and a contemporary of St. Anselm, wrote a reply "In Behalf of the Fool" in which he applied the reasoning to "the most perfect island" and derived the consequence that there exists an island such that no more perfect island can be conceived. In his retort Anselm, whose inspiration seemed to have left him, pointed out that one of the conditions (made clear in the second version above) left unfulfilled by any island is that it is not such that it cannot be thought of as not-existing; for any real island will be part of the physical world and like the whole world of

1960), has supported Anselm vigorously, though he takes considerable liberty with Anselm's text and treats "necessary existence" as a special predicate. The paper was variously and inconsistently criticized in a flock of rejoiners, some of which appeared a year later in the same journal. Others have floated to the surface in other journals since then. See the indices of *The Monist, The Review of Metaphysics, Journal of Philosophy, Theoria, Mind,* etc. Especially see: A. Plantinga (editor), *The Ontological Argument* (New York, Doubleday, 1965).

nature can be conceived not-to-exist. He could also have added that the very nature of the qualities of an island requires that they be realized in space and time and therefore that they could conceivably be improved. A physical object so perfect that it could not be surpassed is like the largest number—impossible. Hence, "the perfect island" is not a legitimate counter-example to Anselm's reasoning because it is inconsistent in itself.

St. Thomas Aquinas opposed Anselm, saying that the mere fact that a really existing thing identical with the-most-perfect-conceivable-thing *would* be more perfect than such a thing existing-only-in-the-mind does not show that such a being exists: ". . . yet, granted that everyone understands that by the name God is meant something than which nothing greater can be thought, nevertheless it does not follow that he understands that what the name designates actually exists but only that it exists mentally. Nor can it be argued that it actually exists unless it is admitted that there actually exists something than which nothing greater can be thought; and this is precisely what is not admitted by those that hold that God does not exist."[4]

Immanuel Kant (1724–1804) in his critique of Anselm's argument insists that the necessities of

---

[4] St. Thomas Aquinas, *Summa Theologica*, I.,q.2, art.1, reply to Objection 2. See *Introduction to St. Thomas Aquinas*, edited by Anton C. Pegis, Modern Library, New York, 1948, p. 22. The reason why Aquinas' meaning is not fully clear is that he is not *directly* examining Anselm's argument but, rather, is replying to the contention that "God exists" is a self-evident truth because God, that than which nothing greater can be conceived, has existence essentially. Aquinas is primarily concentrating upon showing that the conclusion is not self-evident. Apparently, St. Thomas never addressed the Anselmian argument as a simple attempt to demonstrate the truth of its conclusion and no more.

thought are not always necessities of reality apart from the way we think of it. Hence, the whole principle of the second version of Anselm is unacceptable to him. Kant objected with the now-famous dictum that existence is not a predicate. To say that something exists is not to say anything more about what or of what sort it is than we could have said *without* saying whether or not it exists. But to say that something is red or a triangle is indeed to say something about what or of what sort it is. If a predicate is that through which we indicate what or of what sort something is, then existence is not a predicate. Kant concludes that to assert that something exists is merely to *apply* our concepts of what or of what-sort-it-is to the world.

Now what the force of this objection is has never been fully clear, though it is obviously intended to reject the assumption of Anselm's first version: that of two things, *a* and *b*, exactly alike in all respects except that *a* does and *b* does not exist, *a* is more perfect than *b*. If Kant intended to argue that the perfection of the being is entirely conferred by its predicates, by whatever determines what or of what sort it is, then he would indeed be effectively objecting to Anselm. This is perhaps why Norman Malcolm introduced the predicate "necessary existence" into his explanation of the second forms of Anselm's argument (see footnote 3 above); for that predicate would appear to determine what sort of thing we are dealing with and would distinguish it from things of other sorts. Thus Kant may very well be right that existence is not a predicate. Is Norman Malcolm right in saying that necessary-existence *is* a predicate?

The dispute over whether existence is a predicate and over whether or not something which exists is more perfect than something which, though otherwise identical, does not exist has led by way of the second form of Anselm's argument to a dispute over whether something can exist necessarily (be such that it could not have failed to exist). David Hume contended (in both his *Treatise on Human Nature* and his *Dialogues Concerning Natural Religion*) that nothing can be thought to exist which cannot also be thought not to exist (thus denying one of Anselm's premises in the second form of argument above); and, therefore, that no existential conclusion can be derived from a set of premises all of whose members are *a priori*. A great number of writers and countless students have said "Anselm's premises are a combination of definitions and tautologies (necessary or analytic truths); they are intended to be *a priori*; therefore, his existential conclusion does not follow."

But this is just too facile. For one thing, the *denial* of an existential statement can easily be shown to follow from necessary premises and definitions:

a. A square circle is something both square and not square (a definition).
b. Whatever is both square and not square, does not exist.
c. Therefore, it is false that there is a square circle.

Therefore, the negation of the conclusion (the double negation of an existential statement) follows logically from the appropriate negation of one of the premises (conjoined with the others). For example, negate (b) and you can derive the negation of (c) from (a) and negated (b). But the negation of (c) is a double negation of an existential and by the rules of logic is equivalent to the assertion, to the affirmative existential.

Hence, Hume's objection boils down to the claim

that an affirmative existential conclusion does not follow logically from *true* premises which are definitions or *a priori* alone.

But this is doubtful on two grounds: (a) it begs the question against Anselm and others by amounting to an unsupported denial that his premises are true, a denial undefended by any independent reasoning for thinking that they are not true; (b) in purely formal systems such as Russell's *Principia Mathematica* some particular existential statements do follow logically from premises which are either definitions or axiomatic (treated as necessary truths). Hence, it is by no means clear that Hume was right. Moreover, when we consider Spinoza's argument, below, we will see that if we take the Principle of Sufficient Reason as a necessary truth, an existential conclusion can indeed be derived from analytic premises. This rejection of Hume's contention is additionally supported by the Modal Argument we shall describe which uses a much weaker premise than the embattled sufficient reason principle, yet still results in an existential conclusion from *a priori* premises. Hume's position finally turns out to be the simple denial of the truth of his opponents' premises and, therefore, begs the question.

We take the unresolved controversy over St. Anselm's arguments no further, since it should be your delight to develop your own defense or critique of it, perhaps in consultation with some of the vast literature surrounding it.

The question of whether there can be some existent which has its existence by virtue of what it is and which thus exists necessarily is of the greatest importance to philosophy. Anselm, Avicenna, Aquinas, Maimonides, Duns Scotus, Spinoza and Leibniz are committed to the affirmative; Hume, Kant, Locke, Russell and many more to the negative. The issues involved touch upon logic, theory of knowledge, and metaphysics, and will tax your utmost resources.

St. Thomas Aquinas (1224–1274): The Five Ways

In his vast *Summa Theologica* (three quarto volumes), St. Thomas devotes about two pages to a sketch of five arguments to prove the existence of the being which is God. He later takes up the explication of the divine characteristics and the identification of the being whose existence he proves in considerable detail.

We shall not discuss, among those five arguments, the First Way, which is taken largely from Aristotle's proof that there is a first unmoved mover who originates all the motion in the physical world; nor shall we discuss the Fourth Way which is Neoplatonic (Augustinian) in spirit. Rather, we shall concentrate upon the other three.

Each of St. Thomas' arguments begins with the citation of some obvious fact about the world—that some things are moved; that some things are caused to begin to exist; that some things depend upon others; that there are degrees of beauty and goodness; and that natural things regularly behave as if seeking some goal. He then argues that these facts could not be accounted for if there were no first mover, uncaused cause, necessary being, perfect being, or cosmic designer. The body of each proof consists of his reasons why these facts could not be accounted for if his conclusions were false. I shall summarize and explain the three representative arguments before commenting upon their soundness.

The Second Way
1. Some things stand in an (essential) ordering of efficient causes.

2. Nothing can be an efficient cause of its own being.
3. A series of essentially ordered causes of being cannot be infinite.
4. Therefore, there is a first efficient cause (which is uncaused).

Explanation: Any efficient cause is a cause independent in being from its effect; it is an *external* producer of an effect. (The artist, given his equipment, is efficient cause of his work of art). A series of causes can be ordered in various ways—e.g., temporally, spatially, etc. It can sometimes be ordered according to dependence, such that a given member cannot produce its effect except when and while under the influence of the cause which precedes it; the effect is dependent in being upon its cause. Thus, in a stack of bricks the one which holds up the top one exercises its causality in holding the top one where it is only by virtue of the fact that the bricks under it are holding it up, and so on down through the whole stack. Such an ordering of causality is an essential ordering. Some things are brought into being by a series of causes each of which acts in virtue of that which effects and causes its own being. Take the whole set of things upon which your being now depends, and all the things upon which their being depends. Can the sequence be infinite? They would have to exist *simultaneously*. Does it seem likely that an infinite number of things interdependently ordered and without temporal predecessors now exist and sustain you? It is like the story where a boy asks what holds up the world. He is told "Atlas." What holds up Atlas? "He is standing on the back of a turtle." What holds the turtle? "He is in the water." What holds up the water? "It is water all the way down." To where? How tall and long would a brick wall be where *every* brick is held up by adjacent bricks below and beside it? Is such a wall possible? What could account for it?

The Third Way

1. Some things are such that both to be and not-to-be are possible for them.
2. It is impossible for these things always to exist.
3. If everything can not-be, then at one time there was nothing.
4. If at one time nothing existed, nothing would now exist.
5. If at one time nothing existed, it would be impossible for anything to begin to exist.
6. Therefore, not all things can not-be (and some things can begin to exist.)
7. Therefore, something exists which cannot not-be and has this attribute of itself.

Explanation: The terms of this argument are clear enough, but its logic may not be. The things which are capable of not-existing are all thought to begin to exist and therefore at some time not-to-be. St. Thomas assumes that if for each thing there is a time when it does not exist, then there is a time at which no thing exists. (Do you think this is logically sound; if not, why not?) The procedure is then to work backwards: some things begin to exist (they do); it is false that at one time nothing existed; therefore the antecedent of (3) "everything can not-be" must be false; so not everything can not-be; thus, we arrive at (6).

The basic idea behind this argument is that if we assumed that all existence is contingent, there can and could have been nothing which really explains why anything at all exists; the philosophical search for an explanation of the being of things will have been abandoned at the outset and the universe must be acknowledged to be irrational—the latter course appearing utterly incredible and an abandonment of philosophy (which is a search for explanations) to St. Thomas.

The Fifth Way: Governance

1. Some things which lack knowledge act for an end. (This is obvious from their regularity and adaptation.)
2. They achieve these ends not fortuitously, not by chance, but designedly. Otherwise, they would not be "adapted."
3. Whatever lacks knowledge cannot move toward an end unless it be directed by something endowed with knowledge and intelligence.
4. Therefore, some intelligent being exists by whom all natural things are directed to their ends.

Explanation: This is an argument, basically, that regularity of behavior (adaptation) in diverse environments requires an explanation; that goal-directed activity must ultimately be explained through an intelligence. Chance cannot account for the degree of regularity with which the welfare of individuals is achieved in the universe; the alternative to chance is purpose. The natural agents in question are incapable of purpose, despite their purposive acts (acts done *as if* on purpose). Therefore, the purposing agent lies outside them, as does the archer, his arrow. The cosmic purposer, or governor, is the being which is God.

You must distinguish this argument, based upon the regularity of goal-directed action to benefit individual agents and to benefit the species, from the so-called "design" arguments which are based upon analogies as to the origin of complex things (as we shall mention below). The principles in question are significantly different. While it has been traditional since the time of Kant to call those analogy arguments "teleological arguments" (that is, arguments based upon the descrying of purpose in things), this fifth way of St. Thomas Aquinas is actually the paradigm of a *teleological argument*, since it is entirely based upon the question of how we can explain the existence of goal-directed activity. The "design argument" that we shall discuss later (which is usually but inappropriately called "teleological") is more properly treated in the context of arguments by analogy.

Comments: Both the Second and Fifth Ways contain an elementary logical fallacy: a quantifier reversal. From the fact that every series of essentially ordered efficient causes must have a first cause, it does not follow that there is one first cause for all series of essentially ordered causes; from the fact that for every nonintelligent being which acts purposively, there must be a purposing being, it does not follow that there is one purposing being for all purposive agents. This is like saying that just because every mistress has a lover, so there is someone who is the lover for every mistress. The inference cannot be justified on logical grounds.

However a logical defect of this sort can, as you learned in your logic course, always be repaired through quite trivial steps: by introducing an additional premise, for instance, that whenever there is a first uncaused cause in one series of essentially ordered causes, this being is identical with the first uncaused cause in any other series which is actual. Thus, logical mistakes are important only insofar as they reveal how the assumptions of the argument must be augmented. The actual repair of such defects is always a triviality for a skilled logician. Hence, we shall not concentrate on the logical form of the arguments, about which St. Thomas may have taken no special trouble, but rather upon the content. For those additional premises are often obviously false or such as to beg the whole question we set out to decide.

The heart of the Second Way is that the elements of a series of essentially ordered causes cannot be infinite. St. Thomas says: ". . . in efficient causes, it is not possible to go on to infinity because in all efficient causes following in order, the first is cause of the intermediate cause, the intermediate cause is cause of the ultimate cause, whether the intermediate cause be several, or only one. Now to take away the cause is to take away the effect. Therefore if there be no first cause among efficient causes, there will be no ultimate, or intermediate causes. But if in efficient causes it is possible to go on to infinity, there will be no first efficient cause; therefore *neither will there be an ultimate effect, nor any intermediate efficient causes*; all of which is plainly false. Therefore, it is necessary to admit a first efficient cause, to which everyone gives the name 'God.' "

St. Thomas' main reason why the series of efficient causes cannot be infinite is that in the infinite set there will be no first efficient cause, as I have italicized in the passage quoted. He finds that consideration decisive because he thinks he can prove that *if there were no first efficient cause, there could be no efficient causes at all.* And he thinks it absolutely obvious that there are some efficient causes. Thus by negating the consequent of the last conditional and applying the logical rule *modus tollens* (inference from the falsity of the consequent to the falsity of the antecedent), he concludes that there is no infinite series of efficient causes.

With this argument we must learn something new about philosophical method. St. Thomas makes what appears to us now as an elementary mistake about the nature of an infinite series; as a result, one of his key premises is false. If we wished to be superficial, we could note that falsity and then drop his argument from consideration. But we can also add "What would the argument be like, if altered to take account of what we know, which St. Thomas did not know?" In this case I will carry the investigation a step or two further to show you what could be done. You can then go forward on your own with the steps and countersteps connected with the other points considered.

St. Thomas did not know that there can be infinite series which have both a first and a last member. (Can you name one? Can you who have the advantage of seven centuries over Aquinas, show that there must be such a series?)[5] Hence, St. Thomas was wrong to say "if in efficient causes it is possible to go on to infinity, there will be no first efficient cause." If the series is ordered appropriately, there might very well be a first efficient cause in an infinite series. But, what did Aquinas primarily want to say? He wanted to say that there cannot be a chain of efficient causes, whether finite or infinite, which lacks a first member, uncaused by any other in that chain. Anybody can argue this on the ground that the casual activity in the later elements of the series of essentially ordered causes is dependent on the simultaneous activity of everything that precedes it. If the activity of the combined preceding members is not accounted for by the fact that they include one member which is uncaused by any cause, then the activity of the combined preceding members is not accounted for at all or is accounted for by some cause not in the series. In the latter case, there is an uncaused first cause of the series which is not a member of the series. In the former there is no

[5] I have in mind the set of all real numbers between 1 and 2, or the number of points between and including an arbitrarily selected *A* and *B* on a line segment. Both series have first and last numbers, and yet an infinity of elements.

explanation for the existence and activity of the causes in the series, and in fact the causes in the series are impossible. So we find basic to Aquinas' argument this conviction (shared by most philosophers when they are not thinking about philosophy of religion) that for whatever happens in the universe it is in principle possible to give account, to find the explanation. If there were a series of essentially ordered causes in which there was no first member, there would be no accounting to be found for the activity of the later members. Moreover, if the activity of B, C, and D is not possible unless A be acting (as in the definition of series of essentially ordered causes), then if the series be infinitely long, every member must be simultaneously actual and acting and no later subset could be actual if every earlier subset were not actual. These earlier subsets will either contain an uncaused cause or they will not. If they do not, no member of the series is accounted for. St. Thomas thinks this is impossible. The world is not so irrational that there is no account to be given for any of it at all.

He is committed to the view that for any given efficient cause, it either accounts for its own being or is accounted for by something else. Further, by insisting that an infinite series without a first member is impossible, St. Thomas must now say that it is a necessary truth that every efficient cause either accounts for itself or is accounted for by something else. This leads to the fundamental question: Is it *possible* that there is no explanation whatever for the being of anything which exists? How can one show which answer to that question is correct?

The Third Way, given the name "cosmological argument" by Kant who subjected it to a careful critique, is severely criticized by most philosophers and yet is regarded as the argument which has the greatest likelihood of intrinsic merit, but probably

not in its present form. The second premise, that
it is not possible for the things which can be and
also can not-be to exist forever, is a relic of Richard
of St. Victor's saying: "Those things which are eternal are such that it is entirely impossible that they
should not exist . . ." which follows Aristotle: "In
the case of eternal things, what can be must be."
(Aristotle, *The Physics*, Book III, Chapter 4 [203
b, 29]). Most philosophers would see no reason
why this is not false. (But what reason is there for
thinking it is?) For St. Thomas to reason that just
because each thing fails to exist at some time, so
at some time there was nothing, is entirely incorrect. (Why? Remember the example of lovers and
mistresses?) Furthermore, the use of "time" words
is confusing because it is hard to know what "at
one time nothing existed" means since there can be
no time apart from some existence. To say "if at
one time nothing existed, it would be impossible
for anything to begin to exist" is simply to evade
the whole question. If nothing can begin to exist
which doesn't have a cause, then the assumption is
correct. How can we find out for certain that it is
impossible that something should begin to exist even
though nothing existed before it? Four premises of
this argument—2, 3, 4, and 5—appear to be false.

Nevertheless, there may be some merit to this
argument. If you are sure the world is basically explicable, you cannot consistently think that whatever exists is also capable of not-being. For whatever can not-be is incapable of explaining what
there is, because it is incapable of accounting for
its own being. Hence, if any account is possible for
the being of contingent things (the being of things
which can both be and not-be), there must be some
being which is not capable of not-being.

That would be something which would exist necessarily—a being which *is*, of necessity; of neces-

sity—not in relation only to something else, but of necessity in itself: one which exists because of *what* it is and in virtue of its own nature. This point will be elaborated in our discussion of Spinoza's and the Modal arguments.

The Fifth Way assumes that the opposite of entirely random behavior is regular behavior and that regular behavior, behavior which is carried out *as if* on purpose, cannot be accounted for apart from our supposing there to be, ultimately, some purposing intelligence which governs the activities of individuals and species in nature. As the antecedent probability that the individual did what he did by chance (e.g., a bird builds its nest) decreases, the probability of an overall governing intelligence (which probability is the product of the complements of the improbability of chance) increases. Of course, this must premise that there is some accounting for the state of the universe which, in principle at least, can be found. In fact, St. Thomas thinks it is impossible that nonrandom, goal-directed activity should occur regularly and not be accounted for by some directing intelligence, because he thinks that if it is not accounted for by some directing intelligence, it cannot be accounted for at all. Now if you could show this belief to be true, then you would have the whole matter at rock bottom. Can things be accounted for or not? (I will show you later on why this is a rock-bottom issue.) If they can, then there must be a divine intelligence directing the universe and it must be a being which cannot not-be. If things cannot be accounted for, there may be no such being as God is and surely we can never show that there is such a being—how would we ever reason to its existence except as that which is needed to render the world explicable?

We could say to you that if you are willing to

deny that things can be accounted for, then you must justify the enterprises of the physical and biological sciences in terms of their practical results, since the search for the explanation must ultimately be illusory. In fact, you cannot justify inquiries into philosophy, since you must think there are no answers to be found. But these considerations are merely designed to make you uneasy, to put you in doubt. Do you really *know* whether Aquinas' assumptions were wrong or right? There are ways to find out whether things, at least in principle, can be accounted for—how would you go about finding out? The merits or defects of the Five Ways are not dependent upon whether or not you see that they have those merits or defects. But the depth of your philosophical understanding is dependent upon your ability to uncover those defects and recognize whatever may be the merits in such reasoning.

Baruch Spinoza (1632–1677): Sufficient Reason

Instead of showing you the versions of the cosmological argument (the Third Way) which are recognized by Leibniz and Locke or the version criticized by Hume; instead of displaying the variations on the causal argument (the Second Way) which were used by Descartes, Locke, and Berkeley, we shall briefly consider an argument put forward by Spinoza. Despite the fact that his conception of God does not at all fit the central Judaic-Christian tradition, but, rather, stems directly from his disagreement with it, his argument can be considered apart from the metaphysical system in which he describes and identifies God.

Argument from Sufficient Reason

1. For whatever is so, and for whatever is not so, there must be a sufficient reason or explanation.

2. It is either so that God exists or it is so that God does not exist.

3. Assume that God does not exist.

4. Then there must be a sufficient reason or explanation for the nonexistence of God.

5. The sufficient reason or explanation of a state of affairs is either internal to it (to be found in what sort of thing it is) or is external to it (to be found in causes which could produce or prevent it).

6. Nothing can bring it about (through causes producing it or preventing it) either that God exists or that God does not exist; for God is by definition both uncausable and unpreventable.

7. Therefore, the explanation of the nonexistence of God must be found in the very nature of God.

8. But those things which by their natures account for their own nonexistence must be inconsistent and impossible—e.g., square circles.

9. There is nothing inconsistent or impossible about "God exists."

10. Hence, there can be no internal or external sufficient reason for the nonexistence of God; so there can be no sufficient reason at all for the nonexistence of God.

11. Therefore it is not so that God does not exist (from 10 and 1).

12. Hence, God exists, and this is a necessary truth.

Comments: The clarity of the argument allows us to combine comment and explanation. The two key premises are (1) and (9), since the rest are analytic or follow logically from the others (with the exception of the assumption, (3), which is later to be rejected).

The technique of argument is to show that on the assumption that God does not exist, it follows logically that God does exist. Hence the assumption that God does not exist is contradictory and necessarily false, its negation being, therefore, necessarily true. This conforms to the general rule of logic which says that whenever any given proposition Q follows both from some other proposition P and from its negation -P, then Q must be necessarily true.

The force of this argument was so great and it succeeded so well in touching at the center of what had been the great medieval arguments for the existence of God that it inspired several generations of European philosophers, notably Schopenhauer, to treat the Principle of Sufficient Reason (the first premise) as the fundamental principle of metaphysics. Later in this chapter we shall consider the vast ramifications of this principle and especially its paradoxical consequences concerning the relation between God and the world.

For now, let us observe that this principle must be considered not only true, but *necessarily* true, to function as it does in this argument. For the argument to be sound, it must be impossible that anything be so (whether it be that something or another exists or that something or another fails to exist) for which there is not a sufficient reason or explanation (whether or not it be one that we can ever discover). The second key premise (that it is possible that God should exist) is usually not challenged; but it should certainly be noticed and considered.

I will not detract from your pleasure in examining the argument by alleging that it has defects. Instead I will defend it (and the conclusion of the Third Way of St. Thomas as well) against a very common objection among recent philosophers:[6] that it is nonsense to talk of a "necessary being" because only propositions can be logically necessary. There are several good replies to this, but the best seems

---

[6] J.J.C. Smart, "The Existence of God," and J. N. Findlay, "Can God's Existence Be Disproved?" in *New Essays in Philosophical Theology*, Flew and MacIntyre, ed. (The Macmillan Company, New York, 1955), now in paperback.

to be two-fold. First, you can frame the arguments as I have done, *without* talking of "necessary being," by talking only of the logical necessity of the proposition that a being of a certain kind exists. Secondly, you can define the term "necessary being" in a way that is quite intelligible: "*X* is a necessary being if and only if *X* is of such a sort that the proposition that there exists something of that sort is a logically necessary truth." What is nonsensical about that?

That definition has defects (if we do not provide additional restrictions). For, a being which is of sort *S* ("exists necessarily or contingently") because it is *contingent*, will be necessary if any necessary being exists since it will be a necessary being in virtue of the fact that it belongs to a sort *S* such that "there exists something of that sort" is logically necessary. What additional restrictions are needed to straighten this out? (Luckily, this is not the only way to provide the definition we need.)

However, we cannot go on without at least mentioning one key objection to this argument. We shall not, however, discuss Spinoza's reply to this objection since this is more appropriately considered in the context of the Modal Argument. The objection runs as follows: Imagine an uncausable and unpreventable man. Assume that it is possible that an uncausable and unpreventable man exists. And assume that the uncausable and unpreventable man does not exist. If there must be a sufficient reason both for whatever is the case and whatever is not the case, then there must be a sufficient reason for the nonexistence of an uncausable and unpreventable man. But if it is possible for the uncausable and unpreventable to exist, then the sufficient reason for the nonexistence of such a being cannot be internal to it. Yet the sufficient reason for the nonexistence of such a being cannot be external to it either, since it is uncausable and unpreventable. Therefore there cannot be a sufficient reason for the nonexistence of an uncausable and unpreventable man. Hence the assumption that such a being does not exist is false; and it is a necessary truth that an uncausable and unpreventable man exists.

This objection attempts to draw an exact parallel between the form of argument used by Spinoza and an argument involving the existence of an uncausable and unpreventable man. It directs our attention to the fundamental issues. However, while it is generally taken without question that it is possible that God should exist and should be an uncausable and unpreventable being, it is not generally considered to be possible that there should exist an uncausable and unpreventable man. Is there any reason which you can find to show why this should be doubted? We shall consider this point again.

The Design Argument

This is really a family of arguments which Kant labeled "Teleological Arguments." But as we have said, the designation "teleological" seems to apply appropriately only to the subclass of these arguments which are similar to the Fifth Way of St. Thomas Aquinas and does not appropriately apply to those arguments by analogy which we are going to consider now. Etymologically, "teleology" concerns purpose; "design" concerns intelligence and planning.

The design arguments are usually based upon the analogy between the conjectured origin of natural things and events and the design which originates human products. The analogy usually proceeds by a selective description of nature in which one's attention is drawn to those features of natural events which resemble but vastly surpass (in beauty, order, and subtle contrivance) those characteristic features of human products which best display the intelligence and purpose of the human designer.

This line of reasoning does bear some resemblance to the Fifth Way of St. Thomas, and has definite antecedents in the works of St. Augustine and Plato. Moreover, it is usually the most persuasive line of reasoning adopted by apologists who wish to use appeals to reason to support the claims of religious faith. An excellent epitomization of this line of thought is to be found in William Paley's (1743–1805) *Natural Theology.*[7]

If, while walking in a desert place, I come upon a watch lying in the sand and wonder how this object came to exist, I can either attribute its origin, (its coming to be not its lying here), to chance or to some intelligent purpose. When I examine its intricate structure and find the complexity of gears, springs, and balances, all arranged to serve the intelligent purpose of measuring the passage of time, it is not possible that seeing what it is to be used for (what it is fitted to do), I can attribute the formation of its intricate design to the chance conveyance of blind natural forces and particles selected at random. I am compelled to suppose that someone (some intelligent being) made it.

Now the natural world is more complex and more intricately contrived than any watch. Consider just the structure of the human eye with its self-adjusting lenses, its phenomenal range of sensitivity to color and light intensity, its infinitely complex coordination with the other senses, and the behavior of its nervous and kinesthetic systems. And the eye is but a small element of the human body, which is in turn just a speck among the similarly intricate billions

[7] See the edition edited by F. Ferré (New York, Library of Liberal Arts, 1962).

of living things. The earth itself, with all its regularity of behavior, is an infinitesimal part of the celestial systems whose regularity, balance, and beauty are forever a challenge, a standard, and an ideal for human activity.

Can such a vast system of purposes and achievements have come about through chance? Each, even the smallest crystal or living organism, contains countless arrangements of parts which resemble but surpass the greatest achievements of human intelligence. How incredible and improbable it would be that any single part arose from chance! And what of the inexorability of the laws of nature? *Is it a matter of chance that the universe must run down?* Is it a matter of chance that the speed of light is fixed as it is, and that the force of gravity is fundamental and all-encompassing? Is it a matter of chance that the natural laws and universal constants will remain unchanged for billions of years? How can appeal to chance be used to *explain* the origin of the *necessity* which we observe to govern the behavior of natural things everywhere? We must if we think an explanation possible, postulate an intelligent being, an intelligence indescribably superior to our own, whose purposes all this nature serves, to whom it all is meaningful, by whom it was all designed.

Comments: This line of reasoning was roundly and soundly criticized by David Hume,[8] not in Paley's exact words since his book was some twenty years later than Hume's, but in a sufficiently similar form.

Hume directs our attention to the fact that this is an argument by *analogy* to the existence of a certain kind of cause. All such arguments, he says,

[8] David Hume, *Dialogues Concerning Natural Religion*, through Section VIII (New York, Hafner Library of World Classics, 1960, ed. with Introduction by Henry D. Aiken).

are based upon a dual principle: (a) similar effects proceed from similar causes and (b) similar causes produce similar effects. He is willing to grant the principle, for the sake of argument, but cautions that it can be used against the argument insofar as the effect we are concerned with (the observable universe) is similar to the effects of causes quite different from human intelligent ones.

Naturally, he observes, the universe has the *appearance* of design; any universe would, because no great multiplicity of similar things could coexist without considerable adaptation. Of course, Paley would agree and would, however, add that this shows that no physical universe could originate without an intelligent designer since the "product" of any other source would never get going or would quickly destroy itself. But Hume calls attention to the Epicurean hypothesis that the universe originated with an infinite number of indestructible atoms falling in a vacuum, which atoms began to interact through chance and which, if given a long enough time will pass through all arrangements, thus exactly duplicating the history of our own universe. Perhaps, he says, that was the actual origin of our universe. Paley did not have the scientific knowledge we now have to show that there are and can be no "indestructible atoms" and that the Epicurean hypothesis has less merit than the design hypothesis. While the latter may appear to be somewhat improbable, the former is impossible (because of its incompatibility with the actual achievements of physical science).

But Hume did not rest his case upon a single alternative; he suggested that the universe could also be compared to a living being, an animal (as Plato suggested in his *Timaeus*), and therefore could be said to originate through generation from some other living being: the universe might have had parents! The world is as much unlike the product of intelligence as it is like such products, and therefore the conclusion of the argument is at best no more likely than its opposite. For it is merely a postulate, perhaps originating in our anthropomorphism, that those vast parts of the universe which we have not observed are orderly in the way the parts we have observed are. We know too little of the overall structure of the universe to draw a reliable analogy to intelligent artifacts.

Moreover, are we taking the principle "like effects are produced by like causes" to be necessarily true? What is absurd about denying that? But if we take it only to be a general truth confirmed in our observation, how do we know that the universe as a whole is not the chief counter-instance which renders that principle false as a universal truth?

Further, an argument by analogy is never a deductively tight argument; it is always an argument based upon likelihoods. If we have adequately described the overall structure of the universe (something we can never know), then there is some probability (based upon the analogy) that it is intelligently designed: but there is no logical necessity that it has been so designed. It is not logically impossible that such a universe so described arose by chance; it is just "unlikely." "The unlikely" often happens, but not most of the time.

Well, we need not go through the whole arsenal of devices used to attack this argument. It is certainly not a philosophical establishment of the existence of God. And yet, as we shall mention later, it is the line of reasoning which is most useful (of the various kinds of abstract reasoning) in the creation of "nonphilosophical" belief in the existence of God. We shall not debate the most reasonable reply Paley can offer: that he was *not* arguing by analogy but merely pointing out those features in biological nature which exactly parallel (but surpass) those very features we remark in human artifacts and without any question or suspicion of unreasonableness take as grounds for our belief that what we observe really is an object of intelligent design. In effect, if belief grounded on such recognized features of objects is a way to knowledge for most men most of the time, why is it not equally legitimate to use exactly parallel considerations to ground our belief in God, the cosmic designer?[9]

The Moral Argument

Seldom articulated, and then poorly, this line of reasoning is often mentioned and occasionally appealed to by apologists.[10] It assumes that there are norms of right conduct which are independent of human choice or convention, norms which unconditionally impose themselves upon those rational creatures who understand them. These moral laws seem to express an inexorable and entirely sovereign will, a source of command entirely independent of human thought and construction. We simply cannot construe these laws out of existence. What could

[9] For a detailed and highly sophisticated discussion of the design argument, see Alvin Plantinga, *God and Other Minds* (Ithaca, New York, Cornell University Press, 1967).

[10] We find traces of the reasoning in J. Henry Newman, *A Grammar of Assent*, C. F. Harrold, ed. (New York, David McKay Co., 1967). There is a definite appeal to such considerations in Immanuel Kant, *Critique of Practical Reasoning*, Book 2, Chapter 2, Sections 4 and 5. St. Augustine also argues this way (see *On Free Choice*). Strong supporters of this argument were W. R. Sorley (1855–1935) of Cambridge University in *Moral Values and the Idea of God*, 3rd edition (Cambridge University Press, 1919), and H. Rashdall (1858–1924) of Oxford University, in *The Theory of Good and Evil* (London, Oxford University Press, 1924). See the Abernethy and Langford selections (noted in the Bibliography) for Sorley's statement of the argument.

possibly be the explanation for the being of such laws? Not human thought, for we would often change these laws if we could; not inanimate nature, for a rational imperative cannot be produced by unthinking things. The laws perdure while individuals perish. They bind the rational species through the individuals but are imposed inwardly, not through heredity or environment. No explanation of the existence of universal, eternal, inexorable moral laws can be excogitated unless it be that they are the result of the will of a sovereign and unlimited being. The laws exist; so must the sovereign legislator. (We find this reasoning as early as St. Augustine; it appears in Kant; John H. Newman approved it; so have many more recent theologians.)

Comments: The three main assumptions of the argument are: (a) that universal, eternal and inexorable moral laws really do exist and exist independently of any individual's acknowledgment of them; (b) that there must be an explanation of the existence of such moral law; and (c) that the explanation of the existence of such laws cannot be found in inanimate nature, or anywhere in nature at the level of perishable, rational things.

Criticisms of these reasonings are by no means standard. But generally they take the form "How do you know that?" This is because it is somewhat doubtful that anyone really does know that there are universal, eternal and inexorable moral laws which bind all rational beings. Similar questions may be raised concerning the other two assumptions, particularly the assumption that there must be an explanation for the existence of these laws, if there are any. And at least in the case of the first assumption, some evidence can actually be cited to show that no specific moral law does bind everyone under all imaginable conditions. However, what of the law "Do what you believe to be required and avoid what you think to be forbidden"? Does this apply under all circumstances to everyone? Are there such moral laws as the arguments suppose? If you think there are, then in what do you think the explanation to such laws may legitimately be found? And if you do not think that an explanation for such laws may legitimately be found, why not?

The Modal Arguments

There is another group of arguments for the existence of God, ultimately stemming from St. Anselm, Richard of St. Victor and the Arabian philosopher Avicenna. The most sophisticated medieval proponent of these arguments is John Duns Scotus who lived in the late thirteenth century. As late as the eighteenth century, we find these views endorsed by Leibniz. Recently, Charles Hartshorne, an American, has offered very effective interpretations of St. Anselm's arguments on this model.[11]

Basically, the procedure is to argue that "if God is possible, then God exists" (as Leibniz actually said). An immense variety of these arguments is possible, and the technological detail of the more careful ones is formidable.[12] We shall consider a representative of the type quite informally, but fully aware that we may be ignoring its subtleties by treating it without the full-scale apparatus of formal modal logic (the logic of "possibility" and "necessity"). The way the argument proceeds is to assume both that it is possible that God does exist

[11] See works cited in footnote 3.
[12] See Chapter III of my *Philosophical Theology*, Bobbs-Merrill Co. Inc., New York, 1969.

and that God in fact does not exist (as did Spinoza) and, then, by means of various analytic and necessary truths to derive the conclusion that it is not possible that God should exist. This by *modus tollens* is sufficient demonstration that if God is possible, God does exist. That God is possible (that it is possible, i.e., consistent, that an omnipotent, eternal, good, omnipresent, omniscient, etc., being exists) is taken for granted as an initial premise. Consider the following simplified versions of this reasoning, which I have created by altering Spinoza's argument slightly.

1. It is possible that God should exist.
2. Assume that God does not exist.
3. It is either necessarily true or contingently true that God does not exist. (For whatever is true is true necessarily or contingently).
4. It cannot be contingently true that God does not exist, because:
   a) For any contingent but actual state of affairs, it is logically possible that there exists or existed (or will exist or might have existed) some other state of affairs which would have caused it or prevented it.
   b) But, it is not logically possible that there should be some state of affairs logically distinct from "God exists" which could have caused it or prevented it.
   c) Therefore, if "God does not exist" is the actual state of affairs, it is not a contingent state of affairs.
5. Therefore, it is necessarily true that God does not exist. (By disjunctive syllogism of *4c* and *3*; since by 3, if it is not contingently true, it must be necessarily true.
6. Therefore, "It is possible that God should exist" is not *logically compatible* with "God does not exist." For if the latter is true, it is true necessarily; and so too, with the former. But

"Necessarily God does not exist" is directly incompatible with "Possibly God does exist" since "possibly" means "not necessarily . . . not . . ."

7. Hence, lines *1* and *2* are incompatible. But line *1* is true; therefore the negation of *2* is true. Moreover, line *1* is necessarily true. Therefore the negation of *2* is necessarily true. Therefore God exists and exists necessarily.

Comments: Variations upon this form of argument are, at least in principle, endless. The heart of the whole process is in lines 3 to 5 in which it is first argued that the denial of the desired conclusion is either necessary or contingent, as all truths are supposed to be. Then the key step, in line 4a, is to introduce a general condition which holds for all contingent truths—which, however, cannot be fulfilled by the denial of the desired conclusion. We then displayed the incompatibility of the falsity of the conclusion with the premised (line 1) consistency of the conclusion we want.

The recipe is thus, in principle, quite simple. The form is logically impeccable and it is only a matter of strategy to select a proper premise—e.g., 4a, which will place a condition upon contingency which cannot be satisfied either by the proposition "God exists" or by the proposition "God does not exist."

If we had, as does Spinoza, insisted that every contingent but actual state of affairs must actually have an explanation or sufficient reason, we would be confronted with a premise we cannot prove and for which we cannot imagine a single reason which will not beg the question against our conclusion.

But instead of the Principle of Sufficient Reason, these modal arguments use what I call the *Principle of Hetero-explicability*, the principle that for any given contingent state of affairs p, which is not equivalent to the totality of contingent and actual states of affairs, it is logically possible that there be some other contingent state of affairs, q, such that q is related to p as that which causes p to be so or as that which prevents p from being so. A brief examination of our ordinary discourse and of a scientific discourse, too, will disclose that any proposition which we are willing to call logically contingent expresses a state of affairs which we can readily see to be causable or preventable, at least in principle. Hence, the Principle of Hetero-explicability is the more plausible premise from which to begin arguments for the existence of God. It does not commit one to claiming that there is an explanation for every state of affairs. It does not commit one to saying that for any given state of affairs at any given time there actually is an explanation. It merely claims that it is logically possible that any given contingent state of affairs (which is not equivalent to the totality of such states of affairs) has an explanation. There seems to be no reason to doubt this principle. Can you think of a case where it would not hold? A *consistent* case?

We cannot evaluate all the cricitisms and replies which are relevant to these Modal arguments, but we shall mention two: (a) the attempt to reject line 4a, or the Principle of Hetero-explicability by citing a counter-example such as "an uncausable and unpreventable man" and (b) the Kantian objection that an unconditional necessity of thought need not constitute the unconditional necessity of things. To give such counter-examples is to beg the entire question and to complicate things further by raising doubts as to whether it really is consistent that there should exist an uncausable and unpreventable man. For it may well be that on analysis we shall find that the very nature of what a man is requires the producibility and preventability of each individual, and therefore to say "It is possible that there is an unproducible and unpreventable man" is explicitly to contradict yourself. For example, could some rational *animal* be such that it would be inconsistent to say it was generated from animal parents? How?

However, the whole matter is further complicated by our wondering whether there is any relation between the momentary qualities of a thing (for example its *appearing* blue to you) and its dispositions, its modal properties, its *being* blue. To say something is really red is to say something not only about its present, its past, and its future, but, furthermore, to say something about how it would have been had it been otherwise and about how it must have behaved had it been affected in certain ways. Dispositional properties involve modal properties; and surely, uncausability and unpreventability are not "first level" modal properties, but are derived from other modal properties which in turn are exhibited in dispositions which in their turn are recognized through momentary qualities.

As you can see then, whether there can be modal properties and what kinds of modal properties are appropriate to what sorts of things is a very complex matter. The really interesting parts of the philosophy of religion are those places where we have been catapulted beyond our narrow interests into the basic issues of theory of knowledge, metaphysics, logic, or ethics; in this case it is metaphysics which becomes crucial. Do not lightly believe that *nothing* can have modal properties, such as uncausability and unpreventability, which are taken to be characteristics of God; for a resourceful philosopher can show you with great alacrity that modal properties are involved in every dispositional predicate (like hardness, ductility, malleability, etc.) and that the logic or the philosophy which cannot take account of these matters is to that extent, at least, inadequate.

The student who is familiar with Goodman's analysis of "projectibility" in *Fact, Fiction and Forecast*,[13] and with the whole development of discussion concerning counterfactual conditionals (from C. I. Lewis through recent work by Von Wright) will at once observe that even the simplest "physical object" predicates involve logical modalities in their analysis.

In answer specifically to the objection that the same form of argument and the same fourth premise can be used to prove the existence of an uncausable and unpreventable man, provided we assume that such a man is possible—in answer to this objection, we reply: if the premise that an uncausable and unpreventable man is logically consistent, then this form of argument does indeed show that such a man exists. The very fact that the argument shows that such a man exists, suggests that there has been some mistake in conjoining the attributes of unpreventability and humanity. It suggests that, at least as strongly as it impugns the Modal Argument; hence, we must settle that point before we know what to say against the original argument.

In my opinion, the Modal Argument is the most versatile of the proofs for the existence of God. It encourages you to decide just what distinguishes God's existence from the existence of those things which are capable of both being and not-being. It asks you to find the quality of those things which

[13] Nelson Goodman, *Fact, Fiction and Forecast* (University of London, The Athlone Press, London, 1954).

are able both to exist and not-to-exist, by which they have that double capacity, and to see whether that quality is ruled out by our conception of God. If it is, then God must, as Anselm, Maimonides, Aquinas, Scotus, Occam, Leibniz, and Descartes thought, be among those things which can be but cannot not-be. Does it make sense to say "God is a necessary being"? Yes; for it means "God is of such a sort that it is consistent to say 'God exists' but inconsistent to say 'God does not exist.' " That this statement is true is what the Modal Argument purports to show.

Conclusion: Too many philosophers, writing introductory texts, treat the arguments for the existence of God as if they have little to offer the student. They adopt a patronizing, rational agnosticism, apparently equally critical of all the arguments for the existence of God and all those against, an attitude which leads the student to expect little from the whole process of argumentation because he is, in effect, told that at the end of some two thousand years of dispute neither side has made progress.

This is why I have concluded with Spinoza's argument and its transformation into a Modal Argument. The case against these arguments is not at all as clear and decisive as you may be led to believe. Furthermore, there is a great deal to be said in behalf of (as well as against) the classical arguments, even of those of St. Thomas and St. Anselm. But if the student is supposed to decide for or against the existence of God on the basis of these arguments, as they are presented in his introductory text; and if he does not decide for, the arguments are to be considered defective, then what chance do the arguments have? You know very well that as soon as you say you are convinced, someone much more skilled in philosophy than you will call your attention to questions you cannot answer about the premises with the implication that you couldn't have known the premises are true. What then? Will you not conclude that you did not know the premises were true and therefore that you do not see the arguments are sound? In fact, in the confident expectation of such moves and countermoves by those better skilled in philosophy, can you even begin to look at these arguments objectively?

Does the fact that you encountered questions which you could not answer about a given premise or objections to which you find no reply show that you did not know that those premises were true? Not at all! But it may show that you *no longer* know the premises are true. Surely we cannot require that for Jones to know that it is raining he must be able to answer every relevant question about his belief and every objection against his belief! No one could know anything at all. But of course if the questions and objections which you encounter make your belief in your premise waver, then you will have traded, at least in some cases, knowledge for doubt. This is the hazard of education, that some who had few doubts and some truths should work diligently (but not creatively) for several years and finish with many doubts and proportionately fewer truths.

The classical arguments for the existence of God are supposed to carry their conviction in the context of abstract theory, and not in their effect for religious commitment. We know that the premises of any given argument are infinitely analysable, that they can be subjected to an illimitable series of questions and that every question can be answered in more than one way. We cannot expect a person to have gone to the end of an untraversable road in order to have knowledge. Therefore we must grant that that person might, without knowing the answers to various objections to these arguments, and provided these objections do in fact have satisfactory answers, know that the arguments are sound.

The theoretical case for the existence of God is in the very best of health, with new ideas being produced regularly. There is no need to adopt a patronizing agnosticism which says you cannot find out whether or not God exists by means of an argument. You need only say, "We philosophers have not established yet whether God exists, nor have even settled the conditions such arguments must satisfy; yet our attacks upon the matter show definite progress." Isn't this true of every important point in philosophy?

A philosophical problem often has this peculiarity: at any given stage of discussion there are certain known difficulties which any decent answer must meet; but, it is such that each answer which meets the then known difficulties discloses further difficulties which were not seriously anticipated and could not reasonably be foreseen. Hence, it is possible to make continuous progress on such problems without ever reaching a decisive, debate-closing conclusion.

The Psycho-Sociological Objection

The objections to belief in the existence of God which are based upon pyschological, anthropological, and sociological theories as to the origin and function of such beliefs are not as important nowadays as they were a few decades ago. Then they were combined with the belief that all theoretical arguments for the existence of God were irreparably defective, and that no one could have any good reason for thinking that God really did exist. So it was suggested, there is no good reason either from theory or from experience for believing in the existence of God, and every good reason to show that belief in God arose from nonevidential sources. Further, the account of the origin of religious belief offered by these theories disclosed that they were considered to be complete and to exhibit no need for us to postulate an actual diety; hence, the conclusions of the theoretical arguments were thought to be rendered additionally improbable by their being empirically superfluous.

In very general terms, the psycho-sociological theories combine to suggest that out of the complex interplay of individuals and society there develops a tendency of the individual to project human qualities on the large scale. In fact, one might say that what renders man human (exhibits his highest rational qualities) is his projection of all he considers worthwhile upon a plane unlimited—namely, his belief in the existence of an all-powerful, intelligent, good and benevolent God. The theories as to the origins of religious belief are therefore not trying to belittle man for imagining God. They gladly admit the nobility of the conception; they merely suggest that this projection does not arise out of an experience with God but rather arises in another way: through the experience of the embracing society[14] which is ideated as a projection. The basic experiences associated with religion are awe, wonder, the sense of the presence of the holy, the feeling of unconditional moral obligation. All can be accounted for in one's experience of the society in which one lives.

[14] Emile Durkheim, *The Elementary Forms of the Religious Life* (London, Allen and Unwin, 1915).

We need not trace this or the various anthropological theories out in detail because they all exhibit the same structure and are subjected to criticism in the same way. First, one naturally asks whether the theory in question really does explain the origin of religion as a social institution. Does it really provide a plausible account of the facts we recognize? For example, does it fully explain the fact that religious belief is often the main support of conscience when an individual is moved to act *against* his society? The theory which identifies a society as whatever reality underlies a man's conception of God cannot account for the fact that the prophets who act against the trend of society are paradigm cases of those who claim the support of God. Again, the religious person is often the same as the person who feels a very strong commitment to mankind as a whole, for every individual regardless of his local society: he feels these obligations and acts on them even when the entire interest and pressure of the society which nurtured him opposes. How can the God which sanctions his acts be the same reality as the society which opposes them? Perhaps the theories can, by suitable additions, account for these facts and do so without postulating any really existing divine being. Perhaps—then they should be made to and we should look inquisitively at the additions by which the account is to be completed.

Secondly, even if such theories do accommodate the facts, does this mean that they exclude justified and true belief in the reality of God? Does this mean that they constitute an exclusive explanation of the origin of religious belief? Not at all. Any given set of empirical facts is such that there is always, in principle, an infinite number of differing theories according to which their existence can be explained. Hence, even if God does not exist, man would according to the psycho-sociological theories have his belief in God. But this lends no probability whatever to the hypothesis that God does not exist, it merely lays the ax to the argument that we must postulate the real existence of God in order to account for man's having religious feelings.

Well, what about the fact that the hypothesis that God exists is (or may be) empirically unnecessary? Nothing about it. Perhaps God is "retiring." The mere fact that there should be no empirical state of affairs concerned with religion which we can authenticate and which cannot be explained apart from the supposition that God really exists, may render the existence of God unnecessary as part of the hypothesis for the origin of those beliefs, but it lends no probability whatever to the hypothesis that God does not exist. There is no reason why the existence of God should be a necessary element in any empirical theory. The elements of the world of personal experience may be so beautifully interrelated that for each element there are other elements conditioned to supply a suitable explanation. This is to be expected in the product of a perfect designer.

The same remarks apply to the ingenious hypothesis of Sigmund Freud (1856–1939) as to the psychological progress by which religious belief originates.[15] It may very well be that the forces of nature and of the human mind determine that certain individuals have religious belief. Does that mean that such beliefs cannot be true or cannot be knowledge?

[15] Sigmund Freud, "Moses and Monotheism," "Totem and Taboo," "The Future of an Illusion" to be found in *The Complete Psychological Works of Sigmund Freud,* translated and edited by James Strachey (New York, Liveright Publishing Corporation, 1961).

The mere fact that I would have a certain belief even if it were not true in no way precludes or renders it improbable that it is true, though it does indicate that the fact that I have a belief in no way makes it more likely that it is true than it would be if I did not have such a belief.

I am not suggesting that Freud actually succeeded in accounting for the origin of religious belief, though his work is fertile with insight, but I do suggest that even if he had succeeded this would have no important bearing upon the question of whether the belief is true or false. To infer from the ignoble or irrational origin of belief to its falsity or improbability is to commit the psychogenetic fallacy, the fallacy of assuming that just because we can account (in a nonevidential way) for someone's having a certain belief, his belief is less likely to be true. If anything, just the opposite is more likely, given the fact that on the whole what people believe about the world is true.

The Paradoxical Insufficiency of God

Of all those metaphysicians who took pains to offer proofs for the existence of God, the systematic motivating force was not primarily a desire to befriend or support religion. Rather, they were particularly desirous of discovering a plausible answer to the question "Why is there something rather than nothing at all?" Their interests were theoretical, metaphysical ones, at least as much as they were practical religious ones.

As early as Avicenna it became evident that those things which are by nature (in virtue of what they are) capable both of being and of not-being (as must be everything which begins to exist or ceases to exist) are not such that they in themselves account for their own being. If a thing accounts for its own existing by virtue of what sort of thing it is, then it would not be possible for it not-to-be, since in order for it not to be it would have to cease to be of the sort that it is. In other words, if Socrates were of such a sort (e.g., human) that he existed because of *what* he was, then in order not to exist he would have to become non-human—and this is impossible because Socrates, whether existing or not is, by nature, a human.

If those things which are capable both of being and of not-being are incapable of accounting for their own existence, then if any accounting of the being of such things can be found, it must be found ultimately in something which is not capable both of being and of not-being. (A point St. Anselm made very clear in his second version).

Next, one asserts: it is possible that there is an accounting for the being of everything which exists that is capable both of being and of not-being. If it is possible that there is such an accounting, it must be found in what is incapable of not-being (that is, in something which exists necessarily). Hence, if it is possible that there is such an accounting, then it must be possible that something exists necessarily.

But if it is possible that something exists necessarily, it must be actually the case that something exists necessarily. Why? Because whatever is possible-to-be would exist either contingently or necessarily. Whatever does not exist actually but is possible to be, must exist contingently, if at all. No necessary being can be both possible and not actually existing (for then it would be contingent). But every necessary being is possible. Therefore, every necessary being is actual. Hence as Leibniz, Scotus, and Avicenna saw, from the possibility of a necessary being, its actual or real existence follows logically. Therefore, each and every necessary being actually exists.

This, I hope, looks like a formidable argument for the existence of the being which is God. Further, I hope that it makes clear the ancient objective of the philosophers which was to discover the ultimate accounting for the existence of what there is. Yet, as Spinoza made evident, there are only two ways in which God could both account for the world and produce it. In the one case God produces the world necessarily and by nature (as Spinoza proposed in his own system). In the other, God produces the world through causal agency which is brought into action through His free choice.

In the first case, the being of God would fully account for the world, but at the cost of conflict with our experience. If God exists necessarily and produces the world necessarily, then things could not have been otherwise than the way they are. This certainly conflicts with the fairly widespread conviction among humans that things could have been different (or perhaps should have been). Moreover, this concept of God requires one to abandon the central Judaic-Christian conception of God as a free and benevolent agent who creates because of His goodness. Spinoza's theory about the relation of God to the world leaves God insufficient to preserve our conviction that not everything that happens happens necessarily and leaves God insufficient to act in the way the religious tradition has hypothesized. Thus, according to Spinoza's theory, the very being of God is both necessary and sufficient for the being of everything else; the resulting pantheism and absolute determinism of all things (which does away with free will both of man and of God and makes it most difficult to account for intellectual error and moral responsibility) is incompatible with the way in which the Judaic-Christian tradition assumes that God entirely transcends the natural world in His being and is present eminently in acts of His will and love. In the second case, God is thought to produce the world (a set of contingent beings) through causal agency exercised with free choice. The difficulties with this hypothesis are of two sorts, both of which are baffling. Why did God create a world He did not need? And what is the relation between God and what He created?

We shall devote only two paragraphs to the paradox of the divine motivation. From ancient times it has been said that God created the world "because it is good," "because He is good and chooses to confer being upon other things," "because He wishes to manifest His glory." Granting that these are reasons good enough to explain why God would create something rather than not create at all, they are not at all sufficient to explain why God would create this universe rather than any one of an infinite number of alternatives which lay within His power. Surely, this is not the "best possible world," as Leibniz romantically imagined. An all-powerful and omniscient being could surely surpass this handiwork (which Hume compared to the first bungling attempt of an infant deity who abandoned it to undertake a more mature product later on). St. Thomas Aquinas contended (in his *De Veritate*, q.23, a.4) that for any world God could make, He could make another at least as good (and, hence, rejected Leibniz' proposal four hundred years before the enlightened savant ever imagined it). Nor is this the only possible world. Yet it seems that every reason one could imagine which could sufficiently explain why God created this world rather than any other leads to the consequence that He *could* not have created any other—that this is the only possible world. You would do well to try your own hand at constructing such explanations, keeping a sharp eye for the vicious regress I shall now describe.

Suppose there was a reason which God had in creating this universe rather than any other (even though we cannot think of what it was). He could not have had this reason by nature, in virtue of *what* He is; for then He *must* have followed His reason and could not have failed to create this world (a consequence we wish to avoid). So He must have chosen His reason. But He either chose His reason for some reason or He did not. If He did not, He either has His reason (for choosing His reason for acting) by nature, or came upon it by chance. If He has His reason by nature. He *must* have "chosen" the particular reason for acting that He did choose—then again this is the only possible world.

But if He came upon His reason by chance, neither having chosen the former reason nor having it committed to Him by His nature, then it is evident that the world exists by chance and there is no sufficient explanation of its existence.

On the other hand, if God chose His reason for choosing His reason to act, then either He had a reason for that or He did it by nature or came upon it by chance. If He did it by nature, this is the only possible world. If He did it by chance, there is no sufficient reason for the world.

The result, as you can see now, is that God either chose an infinite number of reasons for-reasons-for-choosing-according-to-a-certain-reason, or He acted randomly, or He acted necessarily. We have premised, having rejected Spinoza, that we will not consider the hypothesis under which God acted necessarily because this requires that all false statements be considered inconsistent. Therefore,

He either acted randomly or according to an infinite number of reasons. In the latter case, if God acted randomly, the being of the world is ultimately unexplained. In the former case, God has to make an infinite number of choices in order to make any choice at all. The result is that a choice precedes every particular reason and ultimately some choice is unaccounted for.

Thus, by asking what God's reasons might have been, through which he selected only one of an infinite number of possibilities, we are apparently led to the conclusion that He could not have created the world according to a reason which He freely chose if it be true that whatever happens is actually accounted for. Does it follow that the world must have come about the way Spinoza imagined it, or that it must have come about by chance, or perhaps, that the hypothesis that there is a necessarily existing Creator is by no means sufficient to account for the being of the world?

The second set of difficulties faced by the Judaic-Christian belief that God freely chose the world is concerned with the relation of God to the world and is closely connected to the points just sketched. Is God really a sufficient explanation for the being of the universe? In a sense, yes; and in a sense, no.

The existing of God is not sufficient for the existence of the created world; otherwise, we would fall into Spinoza's pantheism. In addition to being, God must choose that the finite world should exist—this is absolutely essential to the Judaic-Christian tradition. Hence, the existing of God is a necessary, but not a sufficient condition for the created world. Something else is needed: God's choice that there be such a world. Thus, the sufficient explanation for the being of a finite world is to be sought in God, not in the mere being of God but in God's being and free choice. These two cannot be logi-

cally identical without our again encountering the
paradoxical result that this world could be the only
possible universe.

Now if we assume that God really did surmount
the above reasoning concerning His reasons for creating, then there is to be found in God's being and
choice a sufficient explanation for the being of the
world of finite things. God, who necessarily exists
and is both omniscient and omnipotent, chose that
such things should exist. Fine.

But, suppose we pursue the inquiry in another
way, in the way in which metaphysicians have usually conceived it, as a search for the sufficient reason for the actuality, not of finite things alone, but
of all contingent states of affairs which are actual.
Within the universe so described, in addition to the
contingent but actual state of affairs constituted
by your existence and my existence, there will be
included God's choice that such things be actual.
For it is an essential element of Judaic-Christian tradition that God's choice was free—and therefore that
it is logically contingent that God chose as He did
and not otherwise. Hence, the fact that God chose as
He did must be included within the set of contingent states of affairs for which a sufficient reason
or explanation is required.

Since we have granted that, given God's choice,
if the other states of affairs be actual, we have an
explanation for their having occurred, we have only
one element of the contingent universe for which
we still need a sufficient reason or explanation:
namely, that God chose as He did. What could be
the sufficient explanation or reason for that? It
could be found in only one of two places, the divine
nature which would compel God to choose as He
does, or in the divine will which would not. In fact,
the state of affairs which would account for God's

choosing as He does will be describable either in a necessary proposition or a contingent proposition. If it is describable in a contingent proposition, then it will itself be in need of an explanation. If it is describable in terms of a necessary proposition, then it appears that God's choice could not have been free.

The explanation for God's choosing as He does cannot be found in the divine nature for that would destroy the freedom of God's choice, commit us to Spinoza's pantheism and require that this be the only possible world. Therefore, the explanation must be sought in the divine will which acts freely according to reasons freely selected. This will is a power or disposition. It cannot by its very nature produce a choice or we will again fall into Spinoza's view. Therefore, it must proceed by way of selecting reasons. But each of these selections of reasons will in itself be a contingent actuality and will itself demand a sufficient reason, a prior choice. Unless God has a reason for every reason He has, there is some divine choice for which there is no sufficient reason. In fact, if God's having the reasons He has (for every reason He has) is a contingent state of affairs, then there cannot be a sufficient reason for *every* contingent state of affairs. For all that is left over are necessary states of affairs. And the necessary cannot be the sufficient reason for the actuality of the contingent, since that would destroy the contingency of the contingent. Therefore, while it is possible that for any given contingent state of affairs (which is not equivalent to every contingent state of affairs) there may be or may have been a sufficient reason, it is impossible that there be a sufficient reason for every contingent state of affairs. Hence, the strong version of the Principle of Sufficient Reason is false—and, furthermore, incompatible with the Christian's conception of God's freedom. (How does this conclusion affect St. Thomas' and Spinoza's arguments for the existence of God?)

Paradoxically, we cannot find in God the (actual) sufficient reason for every contingent state of affairs. However well we may explain the being of the universe of finite things, there must always remain in principle and in need of explanation, at least one thing: God's having chosen to create the world. And this remains unaccounted-for not because it is mysterious and surpasses the comprehension of man, as Calvin and many other theologians contended, but because the Principle of Sufficient Reason is false.

Some persons conclude from this that the ancient enterprise of seeking in God (a necessarily existing being) the sufficient reason, explanation, or accounting for the actuality of the contingent universe was an enterprise hopeless and misguided right from the outset. Others point out that these writers should never have employed the "strong" Principles of Sufficient Reason (which yielded the conclusion that there exists a necessary being); they could have attained that same conclusion by starting with a weaker premise. For example, what we have called the Principle of Hetero-explicability which does not require an explanation for every (that is, the entirety taken together) contingent state of affairs to be possible, but only that an explanation be possible of any given contingent state of affairs which is not equivalent to the totality of the contingent and actual. You must make your assessment of the ancient enterprise and its modern variation here and in the Modal Argument. But however you assess it, you cannot deny that it is philosophically productive and resulted in the disclosure of the paradoxical but not absurd insufficiency of the being of God to account for the actuality of what is contingent and actual.

Having devoted considerable attention to the important philosophical and theological theories which are related to the attempt to establish the existence of God, we shall now turn to the examination of nonphilosophical, nontheoretical knowledge of God.

CHAPTER II

Nonphilosophical, Nontheoretical Knowledge of God, His Nature, Purpose, Will, and Actions

WE ARE CONCERNED here with the philosophical examination of the nature of faith and reason and the relations of faith and knowledge. In particular we want to ask whether there is any peculiarity about the relation between religious experience and the resulting faith of religious believers which has definitively separated such experience from the rest of our empirical knowledge.

At no point will we assume that all or even most religious believers would claim to have had religious experiences sufficiently elaborate to justify them in holding their beliefs. We will assume, however, that all, were they to understand the implications of denying it, would say that the humans (e.g., prophets and apostles) chiefly involved in originating the content of their religion did have religious experiences through which they discovered the truths to be proclaimed.

We need not presume that religious humans in significant numbers have "found out for themselves" that any of their religious beliefs are true, in any sense other than that (a) they have found their

beliefs a helpful guide to the conduct of a worthwhile life and (b) they have found their beliefs
to be useful in constructing a coherent view of the
explanation for things.

"Having-found-out-for-oneself" is quite distinct
from "having-taken-it-on-faith" or "having-taken-
someone's-word-for-it." Discovering as a result of a
disciplined and recognizably theoretical investigation that something or another is so is a case of
having-found-out-for-oneself and we may presume
that for the most part, people do not acquire beliefs even in the existence of God through theoretical investigation.

Because philosophical knowledge is theoretical
knowledge, we can say that the belief of the usual
religious believer (even if he is a professional philosopher) is nonphilosophical, nontheoretical. To
call knowledge "nonphilosophical" or "nontheoretical" is not to say anything about its content or subject matter, but rather to say what sort of intellectual activity was *not* followed in its acquisition.
There are no "philosophical" truths, if we classify
truths by content; but there are many truths acquired through philosophy and the knowledge one
so acquires can, in recognition of the process which
originates it, be called "philosophical." There is,
then, nothing esoteric conveyed by our saying
that we are concerned with nonphilosophical and
nontheoretical knowledge of God.

In this chapter, I hope to indicate: (a) that there
is no difficulty concerned with nontheoretical knowledge of God which does not have a direct and
fully generalizable counterpart in all empirical knowledge (Thus, the person who wants to deny the possibility of experiential knowledge of God will, to
be consistent, have to deny the possibility of any
empirical knowledge at all); (b) that a sensitive
awareness of the requirements for knowledge of

God discloses much that is of value for the study of empirical knowledge in general; (c) that attention to the epistemology of religious belief will provide a fruitful counterpart for the debates concerning the meaningfulness of religious claims.

FAITH AND REASON—
DIVERSE SOURCES OF KNOWLEDGE

The traditional conception of the nature of faith and reason and consequences to be drawn therefrom. Since the concept "knowledge" occurs throughout the present discussion, some explanation is relevant. We shall say that someone "knows such and such" or has "knowledge that such and such" only when we suppose there is some *truth* which someone *believes* under circumstances where he has at least sufficient *justification* (through some grounds for believing which he actually has) for his believing it.

This is not a fully satisfactory conception of knowledge, as has been admitted from the time when Plato disclosed that "true and justified belief" is defective as an account of what we mean by "knowledge"; the insufficiencies of this analysis have been further underscored by recent philosophical critics, who have uncovered cases of what we admit to be true and justified belief which we can pretty clearly see are not cases of knowledge. Yet no more adequate explanation is readily available and the deficiencies of this explanation are not, in my opinion, subversive of the points I wish to make here. Moreover, this conception of knowledge is quite close to that which has been employed throughout the history of debate over the relation between faith and reason. The student who wishes an alternative analysis of 'knowledge' may consult R. Chisholm, *Theory of Knowledge* (Englewood Cliffs, N.J., Prentice Hall, 1966). One of the limitations of this analysis is its silence on the subject of "trust" as a source of knowledge.

One's having justification in a belief is constituted by a relation between the grounds that a person has and his having the belief he has. It is not some independent and third reality over and beyond one's belief and one's grounds for belief. Even though we cannot here detail what "being justified" consists in, it should be remarked that it has nothing directly to do with the verifiability or falsifiability of the belief. This is true apart from specialized theories such as that of C. I. Lewis, *An Analysis of Knowledge and Valuation* (Chicago, Open Court, 1962), where a special attempt is made to relate the verifiability of what is believed to the matter of one's justification in believing what one believes. I have emphasized the distinctness of justification and verification in order to bring the student quickly to suspect that the "verifiability" criterion of meaningfulness may be woefully inadequate as a vantage from which to attack religious belief.

It is further to be noticed that among the grounds for belief that a person may have at a particular time, we must include his other beliefs, his sensations, the way things look or seem or feel to him, and, above all, the "perceptual set" through which things take on the look, and feel that they have for him. More will be said on this matter below.

One of the older and widely respected theologies, the scholastic tradition whose best known spokesman is St. Thomas Aquinas, developed the concept "faith" in its relation to "knowledge" in terms which have wide acceptance.

Faith and reason are conceived as mental habits or active tendencies which may result in knowledge.

Faith is the tendency (the active disposition) to trust others either through accepting what they propose for our belief or through acting upon their interpretation of the significance of events in our pursuit of knowledge. Reason is the tendency (the active inclination) to investigate and to find out for oneself.

Acts of faith are particular activities in which one trusts others or trusts to an interpretation of events without resting the whole matter upon the results of one's own inquiry. *Exercises of reason* are direct attempts to discover the truth for oneself through direct perception, inference, induction, experiment, or theoretical explanation. To act on faith, where the action involves "taking someone's word for it," taking something to be so without investigation for oneself, may be (and in a fantastic preponderance of cases, is) a way of acquiring knowledge. It may also be a fertile source of error, where unreasonable; and even where reasonable, but unlucky. (We all know the pity sometimes conveyed when one says, "He's a *trusting* soul.") To what extent is reasonable faith in others a more efficient and reliable avenue to knowledge than one's own investigation? This is something the student should try to establish on his own.

Faith may be classified as "human" or "divine," not in terms of what is believed, but in terms (a) of whom we place our trust in, and (b) whose activity is said to motivate us. This double criterion (which is often applied disjunctively and not conjunctively) sometimes causes confusion, leading one to label the same act as one of human faith and as one of divine faith. For example, if I am moved by God to trust what Smith says, my action is said, according to condition (a), to be one of human faith because it is "faith in a human's report," whereas it can also be said to be one of divine faith, according to condition (b), because it is caused or motivated by a divine agent. Again, if I am moved by the testimony of some person (e.g., a persuasive preacher) to place my trust in God, my act may be called an act of divine faith because it is a decision to trust in God. But these ambiguities once described need confuse no one. The really important sense in which many Christian writers want to say the faith of the individual Christian is "divine" is that the state of trust in God is caused by the intervention of a non-natural event—supernatural grace. Since, grace is said to be a cause of one's having the habit of belief and not a justifying or evidential support for belief, consideration of grace is not relevant to the epistemology of religious belief, but to the psychogenesis of religious belief. Moreover, we know that the natural faith of a child, who trusts his parents as veritable oracles, is acquired through causes which have no immediate connection to the purpose the faith serves; the causes of our belief may be quite distinct from the evidence or grounds for our belief. Thus the distinction between natural and supernatural faith as a distinction in the causes of the habit of trust and in the objects to which the trust is directed is irrelevant to our projected critical appraisal of trust as a means for the acquisition of knowledge.

Human faith is natural. It is natural (a natural need and a natural tendency) for one to trust others and to have trust in the reports of others. (When we trust another, we expect him to act rightly and speak truthfully; when we trust his reports, we additionally expect them to be true, as well as truthful.) We have little or no control over the fact that we, to a surprisingly large extent, trust and have faith in other human beings (though not in all or in many all the time). The acts of trust in others (e.g., when we believe without question that an issue of a newspaper really is for the date which it bears) are not, usually individually elicited but result from the habit of faith: the natural tendency to adopt what others say so long as it is consistent with what we know and what we know of them and insofar as the issue is not one that we have already rated as too important for decision without independent checks and confirmation.

The largest percentage of our knowledge comes to each of us through our habitual trust in the reports, research, and opinions of others whom we take (perhaps by an additional application of faith) to be in a position to know. And we do not require that in order to be in a position to know one must in every case be able to find out for himself. It would be a rare person who could claim to have found out or to have checked (or even to have partially verified) any significant proportion of the things he counts among his knowledge (unless he has adopted an unconventionally restrictive conception of "knowledge" or an uncommonly loose concept of "checking").

St. Thomas Aquinas observed that human faith is an indispensable prerequisite for the acquisition of the immense body of knowledge needed for a full and worthwhile life. You did not find out for yourself that Lincoln was assassinated, that World II was fought in Europe but not in Iceland, that the government prints money, that the two persons you consider your parents really generated you, that you really were born on the day your birth certificate alleges, etc.; yet you would claim to know some of these things and a great deal more, things you neither found out for yourself nor could, even now, reasonably verify for yourself.

In fact, verification which is accurate enough to render the hypothesis you accept (even a really

obvious one) considerably more probable than its
negation is often beyond the realm of the practi-
cably feasible. The number of independent checks
to be performed and their cost in time, effort, and
money would make seeking such verification posi-
tively unreasonable as a practice or way of life. You
would rightly be thought to waste your time and
resources upon tests which are unnecessary. Why unnecessary? Because, on the whole what we would
verify is something we already know without verifying it. Whenever you have justified true belief in
a verifiable hypothesis, the act of verifying it will
do nothing to improve your own epistemic state
(though it may enable you to establish your belief
as a scientific hypothesis or to prove it to someone
else).

All of the knowledge which is prerequisite for a
given person's formation and conduct of a theoretical inquiry must be acquired either through his
personal experience or through his human faith.
Your experience is by its very nature so intimately
connected with your "perceptual sets" and the
biases which precede and organize your experience
(biases and "sets" which were acquired through
your simple human[16] faith as a child and have been
reinforced and molded ever since) that it is prac-
tically meaningless to say experience (as we adults
speak of experience) precedes trust for you. More
probably, the reverse is true.

It is perfectly reasonable, though not always so,
to trust other persons. St. Thomas Aquinas said:

"Now since it is necessary in the common intercourse of men that one person make use of another

---

[16] Among the philosophers I know, George Santayana
seems to have had the clearest grasp of the function of what
he called "animal faith" in the genesis of empirical knowledge. Michael Polanyi, too, seems to weigh this factor
appropriately.

in regard to those items which he cannot provide for himself, he has to stand by the things that another man knows and which he does not know, just as one adheres to what he knows in his own past. As a result, faith is necessary in the intercourse of men, that trust whereby one man believes what another man says. This is the foundation of justice, as Cicero says in his *Offices* (I., 7, 23). This is why there is no lie that is without wrong, for this faith which is so necessary is injured by every instance of lying."—From the *Commentary on De Trinitate* by Boethius.

And from that same book—"Consequently, lest man be without any knowledge whatever of these things, provision was made that he might know divine matters at least by faith."

Unfortunately, specialists in the theory of knowledge have not arrived at a general description of the conditions for reasonable trust in others. We can, therefore, speak only tentatively. For an act of trust to result in knowledge, it seems necessary that: (a) the person we trust should be in a position to know what he claims to know; (b) there be reasonable expectation that he is speaking truthfully; that he be, in fact, so speaking; (c) that what he says or intends to convey for our belief is in fact true; (d) that he succeeds in conveying what he intends; (e) that he has acquired his belief about what he conveys to us by virtue of his having been in a position to come to know. This list is not sufficient, but it will do for now. What defects can you find? Can you repair them?

Can the conditions for that reasonable faith which results in knowledge, which are obviously fulfilled in innumerable acts of human faith, be fulfilled in the case of divine faith? In particular can your child come to know about God by way of his trust in what you and his preachers teach him? If a generally trustworthy person who acquires a belief in the way just described should convey it to another human, the other may by trusting him by acting on human faith, acquire knowledge too. Thus there are two directions to which the philosopher's attention is called at this point: (a) to an examination of the ways in which God can become an object of knowledge through experience and convey some truth to those who encounter Him; (b) to a detailed examination of the teaching tradition of Christianity as a source of knowledge. Basically, the first question is the more important, because the analogy between religious preaching and teaching and the process of handing down information through educational institutions is great enough to suggest that there really is no problem in principle with the hypothesis that most Christians and Jews have indeed acquired knowledge of God by way of a faithful teaching tradition which ultimately originated in the direct confrontation between certain human beings and God. Why could not your child learn in just the way we described?

Hence, beyond some peripheral consideration of an alternate conception of faith and of the matter of conflicts among the results of faith and reason, we shall devote most of our attention to an epistemic examination of religious experience. This topic is important not only because it would make no sense to say one Christian can teach another on the basis of what his elders taught him, if the whole process does not originate in someone's perceptual experiences, but also because a surprising number of our contemporaries claim to have experiential confirmation of those original encounters with God.

It is generally contended by Christian theologians that the nature of the Christian teaching is such that persons are not naturally motivated to trust others that far; no one comes to accept such truths apart from the intervention of God who provides the grace of faith, moving them to believe that what they are told is true and is ultimately conveyed by God Himself. This hypothesis as to the origin of the habit of trust which underlies religious faith does not appear to have been carefully examined or rigorously established. It need not be debated here since it again leads to the psychology of religious faith rather than to its epistemology.

The chain of human testimony must end at the first human or humans to whom the truth was conveyed by God. They were in the position to know. Otherwise, no one they told had knowledge even if God motivated this belief (unless such a person could have found out for himself). They were in a position to know only if the experiences they had were sufficient to give them knowledge. Hence the importance of asking whether religious experience can be a source of knowledge and, in particular, whether the kinds of experiences given the prophets and apostles could have been a source for the knowledge claimed. It is their experiences on which the testimony of church and preaching is founded. If their experiences could and did provide knowledge which they faithfully reported, then those who have reasonably trusted them and trusted to God's acting through them will have knowledge, too.

So far, I have provided only a general idea of what has been involved in the traditional claim that one can through faith come to know God. But what of the people who say religion is not based on knowledge but only upon blind trust?

There have been some theologians and not a few philosophers who have insisted that faith is belief based upon *inadequate* evidence, or no evidence at all; that faith is essentially unjustified belief, the very antithesis of knowledge. C. J. Ducasse, a respected American philosopher, in his *Philosophical Scrutiny of Religion*,[17] speaks thus of faith: "The general sense is belief, perhaps based on some evidence, but very firm, or at least more firm and of more extensive content than the evidence possessed by the believer rationally warrants."

This view ignores two things: (i) that faith is primarily a habit or tendency to trust someone or some source of opinion as well as (and not less than) a tendency to have confidence in someone or something (confidence that someone will act benevolently or that the events will turn out in a beneficial way); and (ii) that faith, both in human persons and institutions and in God can, at least in principle, be a source of knowledge.

Ducasse's opinion radically distinguishes faith from knowledge because a person to have knowledge must actually possess grounds which sufficiently warrant his beliefs, whereas this is just what is said to be lacking in the case of faith. But Ducasse confuses the issue with talk of "what rationally warrants." In the case of empirical knowledge the sufficiency of the evidence of grounds simply cannot be logical sufficiency. It is impossible that in a contingent but true "physical object" belief about the empirical world a person should possess grounds or evidence whose presence is logically incompatible with his belief's being false. Yet whatever the sense of "sufficiency" in which empirical knowledge is "sufficiently grounded," it is clear that the view Ducasse supports must insist that in *that* sense faith is not sufficiently grounded. No evidence whatever is offered to support this. The widespread "inadequate evidence" view of faith is entirely un-

[17] New York, The Rand Press, 1953, pp. 73-4.

faithful to the Scriptural and traditional teaching
of Judaism and Christianity.[18] Moreover, it is inconsistent with the facts we have ascertained about
human faith as a source of knowledge; and it additionally ignores the important distinctions among
the variety of means (rational activities) through
which knowledge may be acquired. Faith is not the
habit of the irrational or the nonrational; it is the
indispensable precursor of every achievement which
advances human knowledge beyond its present.

It is simply false that all knowledge is acquired
through activities whereby a person "finds out for
himself"; little is acquired by any given individual
this way. Most is *transmitted* through others and is
acquired by means of our trust. "Reason" as the
name for the tendencies and activities involved in
finding out for oneself and by oneself is the proper
counterpart of faith which is the habit which occasions our finding out through transmission. Faith is
a requisite disposition on the part of the person to
whom knowledge is to be transmitted.

I call the view we have been discussing a devia-
tion both because it is philosophically inadequate
and because it is alien to the religious tradition to
which it is applied. That conception of faith arose
among philosophers who could see no way in which
to explain how the faith of religious persons, their
preachers, and ultimately their apostles would have
been sufficiently grounded; these philosophers converted the inadequacy of their epistemology into
a constituent of the concept they analyzed.

It should be quite obvious now that if you believe
what is told you by someone who is veracious (a
truth-teller), if you believe because you think he

[18] Faith is also the disposition of persons to expect beneficial results from the acts of others; but this sense of *having
faith in* will not be developed here, despite its importance.
However, the concept turns up later in this Chapter.

knows whereof he speaks, and if he does know, either because he has found out for himself or because he was told by someone (and we can put in as many intermediaries as we like) who found out for himself, then you will have acquired knowledge.

The whole process must necessarily end in the person who is in the position to know and who did know, having found out for himself through empirical knowledge or theoretical investigation. The originators of the religious tradition, the prophets and apostles, did not create the tradition through theoretical investigation. So, if they had knowledge on these matters at all, they acquired it through some "religious" experience. Therefore an adequate analysis of religious experience is fundamental to the philosophical critique of the claims of holy persons to know the person and will of God.

Conflicts of Faith and Reason

If we consider faith and reason primarily as processes by which one may acquire *knowledge*, then genuine conflict cannot result; for whatever is known, regardless of by whom, is true and all truths are compatible (even though they may appear to a narrow estimation or in the short run to be in conflict). This, in a word, is how the followers of St. Thomas Aquinas resolved the question.

If we take faith and reason primarily as processes or habits in accord with which persons *act* more or less successfully in acquiring their beliefs, then it is evident that conflicts in the resulting beliefs can and will arise.

We have already said that one's faith may be more or less reasonably grounded and more or less prudently exercised. So too, reasoning (the process of finding out for oneself, whether through experi-

ence or through theoretical investigation) is based
upon abstractions from experience and can be more
or less sufficiently or successfully conducted. A person may try to find something out for himself and
may think he has succeeded when he has in fact
fallen into error. Reason is not an infallible guide
to truth. Neither is faith. Some people are too trusting; others, too self-confident.

The Judaic-Christian tradition has conceived
faith in the revelation of God in such a way that
faith is the paradigm of a reliable guide to truth.
This is why it has long been claimed that where
there is a conflict between what has been acquired
through religious faith and what is the apparent
result of rational inquiry, the defect must lie in the
exercise of reason. There is in principle no logical
defect in this view. But in practice there are difficulties aplenty, for it was formulated in an age
where few were uncertain as to what faith had disclosed and fewer still considered religious doctrine
to be in development. Now, even the most con-
scientious believers are willing to admit that in
some respects what is taken as faith may undergo
a certain amount of development. There has been
a gradual alteration of thought about the status of
certain parts of Scripture. For example, there has
been a definite revamping of the interpretation of
Genesis. The revision of what is to be taken on faith
is caused by the acquisition of knowledge through
rational inquiry and is also caused by the development of knowledge acquired through the actual life
of the religious community.

The conflict paradigms are cases where persons,
strong in faith, feel compelled to reject some scientific hypothesis which happens to conflict with what
they "know" through faith. The scientific hypothesis
(for example, the biological evolution of man or

the possibility of artificial production of living things) is thus subjected to attack as something pernicious to religion. Time passes and some version of the criticized hypothesis becomes the firmly entrenched scientific theory. Eventually, there comes a time when the religious person begins to reconsider the extent to which he feels his belief on such matters to be attested by divine witness. In the light of the new scientific knowledge, the formulations of belief are reexamined and found to convey elements which were given undue emphasis, elements not central to the belief required and guaranteed. (The so-called "point of affirmation" doctrine in Scriptural studies.) Gradually those elements are abandoned or rephrased and the original belief is recast. Although there is always a narrow-minded segment who insist that such reinterpretation of the Scriptural "faith" constitutes an abandonment of "*the* faith" the largest proportion of believers feel that God has endowed the religious community with a growing consciousness and a developing understanding of things originally committed to man. That the expression of faith should occasionally adjust itself to the achievements of science is neither unexpected nor scandalous.

Sometimes the conflict is resolved in the opposite way—a point not often enough noticed. A scientific hypothesis condemned by Jews or Christians because of its incompatibility with their religious faith is subjected to careful *scientific* criticism and found to be false. We don't especially notice these things because dead scientific hypotheses are usually forgotten or obviously absurd, whereas embattled religious premises become all the harder to dislodge. Those biologists who claim that some races are subhuman and are not equal in rights and dignity with the white race have been castigated by

Jews and Christians alike for teaching falsehoods incompatible with revealed truth. So too, with the Aryan race-supremacy thesis. The progress of science has tended to confirm the falsity of the biological hypotheses, just as it has falsified theories which equated man with the beasts, proposed the disregard of human life and the insignificance of the individual for the social welfare. The religious believers need not wait for the final ax to be applied by science; they already know the outcome. Sometimes science needs to catch up with religion. This has been evident on many occasions in psychology, political theory, economic theory, and sociology. The resolution of the conflicts between the results of reason and faith is a two-way street in which just very slightly the preponderance of concession has, I think, been to the claims of religion. (This surprises you? Think of the many theories of politics, economics, sociology, and psychology which were antithetical to religion, were considered "scientific" and have eventually turned out to be false or useless. Why not list some?)

The products of faith and reason must cohere (be consistent) insofar as they are knowledge. Insofar as they really conflict, they are not knowledge, though both may be reasonable. The religious believer will quite reasonably privilege his religious conviction until the established truth forces him to realize that he overpacked his "revelation." The rational investigator will in his turn privilege his results until the evidence runs against him. Nothing is undesirable about that. But it does become awkward when the two tendencies conjoin within one person. If the person in question is an active, scientific investigator, he cannot simply dismiss the results of his own inquiry just because what he had taken on faith conflicts with it. He must rather consider the possibility that, should his discoveries become the established fact of science, he will have functioned centrally in the development of his historical faith by eliminating a well-entrenched but inadequate understanding of one of its doctrines and, perhaps, by substituting new and clearer concepts. Of course, he must also consider that all too often the entire scientific community has endorsed as truths hypotheses later found absurd. It is thus not the problem of any individual to decide finally and decisively on an apparent conflict between his results and his religious faith. The whole conflict situation has been falsified by those who create too dramatic and individual a setting for it. The conflict is between social institutions (church and science) which must continually adjust to one another but which almost always slip partly out of phase because of the inertia of large groups of individuals. Think of the respectable physicists a century ago who pontificated on the question of God's existence and continued to sputter their denials and assertions long after the leaders of scientific community realized that neither confirmation nor refutation of such hypotheses can ever be expected from the natural sciences. The problems of conflict are unreal. Psychological crises of individuals and inadequate communication among institutions have been mistaken and masqueraded as philosophical puzzles.

When the conflict is within one person, it may be a conflict of faiths—of human faith in the reports of some science and of divine faith in one's religious beliefs; or it may be a conflict of faith and reason, a conflict between transmitted belief and the product of one's own discovery. We cannot follow the path through these difficulties here. You should attempt that, since you have probably experienced the former conflict more than once and may meet the latter soon.

Knowledge Through Religious Experience

Many recent theologians have proposed that it is central to the Judaic-Christian tradition that man encounters God, that each man exists as a "thou" for God and that God can be a "thou" for man. Encounter, the interpenetration of personalities, is possible through religious experience. This doctrine has been popularized to such a degree that individuals often think worship should be associated with some experience (feeling of the holy, sense of the awesome, or perception of the existentially unpredictable) which will give certainty of an encounter with God. And some even claim to have achieved this.

Whether theologians such as Bultman, Buber, and Bonhoeffer expected religious experience to be assigned a central role in the worship of individuals is not clear. But the desire for experience to authenticate the real but nonsubjective encounter which is supposed to occur in communal worship has become common among Western believers. In my opinion it has become too common, holding out false hopes, creating seldom-satisfied expectations and obfuscating the historic role of teaching and preaching in the communication of the message.

Even though the ancient tradition of spiritual writers made less of personal interaction and awareness of God, the proposal that direct experience of God can be acquired is by no means alien. The Biblical prophets claimed to be directly aware of God and of His word; they had religious experiences. Some persons thought they encountered the Messiah and even God in Jesus, though others who met Him did not. These prophets, apostles, and disciples through encounter with God discovered what God wished to have communicated to other men and what God's will was for men. The *function* of the religious experience was to produce a state of revelation which could be transmitted through the preaching of the "Kingdom of God at hand." The function of the experience was to achieve the authoritative declaration of the divine message, not to provide satisfactory religious "fulfillment" to the participant.

It is essential that we distinguish the religious experience in which beliefs about God's existence, nature or actions originate from those experiences which arise from the exercise of prayer in accordance with extant religious belief. Among those for whom religious experiences originate belief there are some who are brought to an existing faith and there are others who are founders or integral developers of a faith, such as the prophets, Jesus, and his disciples. Upon whether or not their experiences provided knowledge, rather than just reasonable but unjustified belief, depends the answer to whether their followers have, in practice, acquired knowledge through faith in their transmitted teachings.

Whether anyone acquires knowledge of God through experience has become additionally important because some philosophers have said (as part of another discussion) that individual Christians have no experiential ground upon which to base their conviction that God is morally good, or for that matter that God exists at all, or that He is omnipotent, etc. They have erroneously concluded that the religious doctrines must be considered meaningless. Particular Christians are inclined to reply, "I don't need to have experience of those things (How could I, anyway?) in order to know that God is good and powerful. I was taught these things by persons who knew what they taught." Could the religious innovators or orginators (Abraham, Moses, Christ, etc.) have known whereof they spoke? They would have to have gained their knowledge through some experience. What experience and how?

When we ask "Could the persons we are concerned with have known whereof they spoke?" we are not interested in mere logical possibilities. The answer would then be "of course they could" and no further argument would be needed. What we want is an explanation or account of the process by which the prophets and apostles may have acquired knowledge, an account which will explain how religious experiences might actually provide knowledge.

The difficulties we encounter are not wholly or even mainly difficulties created by the fact that we are dealing with religious experience. Philosophical achievement in the analysis of empirical knowledge in general has been limited. When we were dealing with theory of knowledge in general, we could have asked for an account of the process by which a person acquires knowledge through sensory experience (any experience at all) and we would have encountered many tangled concepts. Further, the notion of "religious experiences" is of doubtful value; we might just as well ask for an account of a person's coming to the knowledge of God through experience. The adjective "religious" adds nothing beyond a conventional classification of the resulting beliefs and attitudes.

Some writers think "faith in" is religiously a more important concept than "faith that." Epistemologically this seems true, too. The child has faith in his parents. He has on the whole, an unwavering expectation that his parents will do what is good for him and even what he desires. His "trust in" is the emotional motivating ground for his "faith that," for his believing what they tell him. So, with the apostles and prophets. Their faith in God was the inward factor which led them to have "faith that." The disciples of Jesus were men at first of little faith. But when their faith in Jesus grew up from its mustard seed through their wonder at his power, their faith that what Jesus taught was true and all-important, grew apace. Hence, faith in God and in his Messiah was a prerequisite, religiously and epistemologically, to the greater part of "faith that," at least among the innovators and originators of religion. When you lose faith in someone, it will not be long before you lose faith that what he says is so, and when your "faith that" is strained far enough and often enough, you may lose "faith in" too.

Faith in God and in Jesus was undoubtedly an emotional and psychological prerequisite for the religious experiences which originated the doctrinal tradition. If you don't have the right attitude ("faith in"), you may never be able to regard things *as* an encounter with God. Faith in God is generally an emotional predisposition for religious experience. But a religious experience involves several other features: (a) the assignment of significance (i) to the sensory data and (ii) to the perceived elements of the event; (b) the existence of appropriate "perceptual sets" which dispose one to the assignment of significance; (c) the occurrence of disclosure situations in which normal perceptual sets are transcended and new significances are assigned. These terms do not name special elements of religious experience, but rather name features which are fundamental to the structure of all experience and which, when understood, exhibit the community between religious experience and empirical knowledge in general. For instance, not every experience involves a disclosure situation. But the occurrence of disclosures is required for the alteration of perceptual sets, whose alteration, in turn, is required for changes in our significance assignments to become habitual.

Some thinkers have assumed that the belief in miracles, voices, and inner promptings, which accompany the birth of someone's doctrinal convictions, cannot possibly be adequate grounds for the truth of such convictions because no one could ever be sure he really is having the religious experience he thinks he has. You can be sure of your subjective states, perhaps; but of their objective correlate? Visions, miracles, encounters with the holy, and feelings that the eternal is touching you are not part of the daily experience of mankind and they are not testable through experience. So, it is argued, beliefs which arise from and are grounded upon such experiences are not to be called empirical knowledge.

This is surely the most common position of modern philosophers; and while they have not denied that some empirical test might be applied to the given religious belief (for example, we could ask whether most of mankind would feel benefited by having such belief), they argue that such tests are irrelevant to the decisive confirmation or falsification. And, anyway, they would be tests designed to confirm or falsify what was believed by so-and-so on the basis of his experience. They would not be directly relevant to whether he really did have a *perceptual* experience.

How can you test a man's conviction that yesterday at three A.M. while he was entirely alone, he had a vision of God? From some tests we would conclude that he had probably not had such a vision. For example, if tests indicated that he was insane, drunk, or sound asleep—but who knows that God does not appear to the insane, drunk, and those who are asleep? We might even claim that we knew such a man did not have a veridical experience of God. But how could we know that? It is equally obvious that if he did have a veridical experience of God, our tests could never yield knowledge that he had. This creates an interesting puzzle as to when it is reasonable for one to trust the claims of another who bases his claims upon some experience which has not been shared. For example, was it reasonable for the Jews to believe Moses when he announced that he had conversed with God and had been given God's commandments? What are the conditions for reasonable trust in the absence of several participants in the experience which originates the claim?

On the basis of a high estimate of the standards satisfied by empirical knowledge and of a low estimate of the success of religious experience in meeting such standards, religious experience is almost universally considered an unlikely ground for genuine knowledge of God.

In the following, I offer a revision of the high standards for empirical knowledge and of the low estimate of religious experience, with the resulting suggestion that religious experience can indeed be a source of knowledge. This is done by our indicating certain elements common to all perceptual experience and suggesting that there is no reason in principle why events may not have the significance the prophets and apostles assigned to them.

In any case of perception, for example, seeing that Jones is crossing the street, the information we have at hand as a basis for our beliefs (for instance, the information that it looks as if Jones is crossing the street) is of such a sort that we could have had that information and have been wrong in our belief. No matter how much information we have at hand, whenever our knowledge is from experience, the grounds for our belief are logically compatible with the falsity of our belief. This is the basic limitation of empirical knowledge.

The connection of grounds to warranted belief is by way of a perceptual set, a tendency to evaluate and assign significance to sensory clues within a certain pattern, with the result that our "seeing-as" or "regarding-as" step in perception is formed by the perceptual set and passes without alteration into the "taking it to be" stage (provided the expectations aroused by the perceptual set have not as yet been disappointed). We shall briefly explain and illustrate these ideas, with confidence that you will grasp their applications to religious experience.

First, a digression—If you are willing to account nothing true for which you cannot construct a process of verification or falsification, then you will very probably say that "Moses had a vision of God" is something neither true nor false. But most philosophers who have studied the controversy over verification and falsification as necessary conditions for empirical meaningfulness, have concluded that neither can consistently be counted as a necessary condition for truth or falsity. I suggest that those who reject religious experience on the ground that nothing verifiable or falsifiable results, make two mistakes: they ignore the fact sometimes the results *are* verifiable or falsifiable; and they require too much of the bearers of truth or falsity in general when they demand verifiability or falsifiability in every case. The attack upon the meaningfulness of religious belief because it is empirically unverifiable is an abandoned carcass in the morgue of metaphysics under the label "logical positivism."

Suppose we agree that some of the beliefs (regardless of their verifiability or lack of it) which result from religious experiences are true, in what way can the religious experience provide grounds for or warrant the belief that they are?

Significance and "Seeing-as"

In general, the sensory information a person possesses provides a warrant for a given perception only if the sensory information is appropriately assigned significance.

For instance, suppose a native is walking on his deserted beach and comes upon an object which we would see to resemble William Paley's hypothetical watch. The native picks it up and does not know what it is; he throws it away as useless; never having seen a key before, he does not conceive of winding it and has never imagined telling time in anything less than sun movements. In later years he is asked, "Did you ever see a watch before you came to England?" He replies, "No." He is both right and wrong: wrong because there was something he saw which was a watch; right because there was nothing that he saw to be a watch. It may also be true that many men have seen the heavens which declare the glory of God and the firmament which proclaims His power; and that many fewer indeed have seen that the heaven declares the glory of God and the firmament His power. In order to see *that* x is F, you must be inclined to see (regard) x *as* F; seeing-as is the prerequisite for all the more sophisticated forms of seeing-that. The native was utterly unable to see the object as a watch. Hence, he could not see that it was a watch. The native does not end up with false beliefs after holding and observing the watch; he sees it as metal, curious, and unintelligible to him, as a thing in which he descries no function. A watch certainly can be so regarded and thus its appearance has that significance. The native simply fails to assign the whole significance to the data he possesses, and his failure to do that is not a failure of his intellect, but of his environment. He is not rich enough in experiences of the fitness of the things to regard this object as fitted to do anything worthwhile.

Suppose there is more to the case; suppose the watch also has an inscription on the case, the initials: "W. P." The native cannot begin to see the watch as William Paley's watch. He lacks the prerequisite knowledge of inscriptions in general and the knowledge of that one in particular. Hence, he forms no questions as to how it got here from England, etc. Since he could not see it as the particular thing it is (by our hypothesis), he could not imagine the vast set of questions which must be answered to account for its being where it is. To emphasize the difference, you need only imagine that its owner by some freak of circumstances finds it himself.

We cannot go into all important facets of this idea; but let me reiterate that it is essential to empirical knowledge that the perceiver assign proper significance to the preconscious sensory data. (And there is absolutely no reason at all to think that the "proper significance" to be assigned a particular datum is unique!) Thus, for the perceptual experience itself to be "full," the person must assign significance to the experience as a whole. In both cases "assigning proper significance" is primarily indicated by one's knowing what questions to ask or what sorts of checks and expectations are appropriate.

Suppose my wife to be driving home from the store. She hears a curious automotive noise and is finally stalled in the country. When a tow truck driver arrives, he says, "Lady, didn't you hear the radiator boiling over? Why didn't you stop?" She says, "But all I heard was a loud screeching noise and a few whistles; I didn't hear the *radiator* do anything." The physical cause which was there to be heard, went unheard because the sounds lacked significance.

The ability to assign significance is often what differentiates the expert from the neophyte. The "natural" genius is distinguished by his intuitive and uneducated powers at it. The power to reorganize the data, to regard things as different from the way they are commonly regarded is characteristic of the creative imagination and accounts for the discoveries of great originators.

It is the element of significance assignment (ignored in most discussions of empirical knowledge, even by philosophers as distinguished as C. I. Lewis) which converts the apparently irrelevant into the warrant for belief; it transforms a qualitatively empty experience into an appreciation of purpose, beauty, or potentiality. Assigning a significance affects the way the sensory data is manipulated and results in the construction of relations by which the data warrant belief. There has been considerable psychological experiment which confirms not only the fundamental importance of significance assignment but also established the existence of habits of such assignments, called "perceptual sets." The experiments illustrate that what you see is conditioned by the force of perceptual expectation. The student interested in the theory of knowledge or in its applications to aesthetics and religion must not fail to study this literature.

Because we cannot explain this central epistemological point sufficiently in this text, you will have to take it on faith that there really is a great deal to it. Suppose there is. How does it forward our inquiry concerning religious experience?

What is a religious experience? It is an experi-

ence generated out of the assignment of significance
to sensory data that we take ourselves to be aware
of the holy, the presence of God, the words of God,
or some other event which would conventionally be
considered religious.

Is there any reason to deny that the very same
thing that I see (for example, a mountain tra-
versed by a valley and crowned with purple clouds)
may, while it is still data-for-seeing and not yet
seen be assigned significance so that one's mind
is directly conveyed to the presence of God or
of God's will? There is in principle no reason
whatever for our denying this.

The function of perceptual sets here is crucial.
The subject must be actively disposed to assign significance to the phenomena so that it really appears
to him as an experience of God. This is not something you can do for yourself deliberately, though
it is not inconceivable that you could, as a result of
many deliberate acts of attending to details, create
the habit which will bring about the experience.
Some duck hunters, in the company of a neophyte
in the sport, can completely mystify him by their
discussion, in considerable detail, of ducks he cannot even see. Eventually the novice learns at least
to see them as black dots far off in the sky; but
he is well on the way to being an artful hunter before he can see them as mallards or whatever.
Perceptual sets can be created, can be learned and
can be lost. When you lack the requisite set possessed by others with whom you converse, you tend
to be suspicious of them, to think they are "pulling
your leg" or "creating a mystique." When once you
have the set, you find it hard to understand why the
novice fails to see what you see and you are at a loss
as to how to mould his perception.

There are auditory perceptual sets, too. Studying
the theory of equal temperment for piano tuning,

I learned about beats which can be heard and counted and on the basis of which the entire tuning can be rendered objective, precisely testable and quick. Even with the help of a person experienced in the art, I had the greatest difficulty hearing beats and it was an overwhelming obstacle actually to count them (and get the right answers). For a while it was hard to believe there really were such things to be heard. Yet those very sounds were there all along to be heard by one who knew how. So they are for you, too. A whole life of perceptions formerly closed to you becomes available when you have the appropriate perceptual set. You, if you had the art, would assign a new significance to the very same auditory input you now have and would perceive things about the instrument which at present entirely elude you. The complex sound, undifferentiated by the untrained ear, is produced by those distinct sounds any tuner can hear and adjust. With the proper perceptual set, physical objects can be manipulated in ways which remain impossible for the person who lacks it.

It may be argued that although religious experience shares assignment of significance and pre-structuring through perceptual sets with other perceptual experience, it differs in an epistemologically central way: one person cannot have empirical knowledge that another person has had a veridical religious experience. The argument runs as follows:

If you see a chair and report it to me, I can in many cases tell whether or not you did see a chair merely by looking for myself. Even though this is not theoretically sufficient because there are an unlimited number of defeating circumstances (e.g., you may have been mistaken about what you saw, but used the right word "chair" when you meant to say "table"), I do in many cases have empirical or experiential knowledge about your having had a certain veridical experience. Even in aesthetic matters, interpersonal checking is appropriate and successful. If you report that you have noticed that a certain painting is heavily massed and structurally elaborate, I can look for myself to see whether it is so and by determining whether the objective necessary condition of your perceiving (that the object be as you think it is) is fulfilled, can proceed by way of general knowledge of the circumstances of your report, to whether or not yours was a veridical perception. But this does not appear to be so for religious experience. It is not a normal thing for me to be able to check the veridicality of someone else's reports by way of my own experiences of the object or event he claims to have perceived. The interpersonal assessability of most perceptual claims does not seem to belong to reported religious experiences.

This argument oversimplifies the situation which obtained among the originators of the Judaic-Christian religion and between them and their earliest converts. Situations of empirical confirmation were created by the wonderworks of the prophets and by the religious experiences of their converts who, while not given authoritative missions, often claimed to have experienced the Spirit and to exhibit His gifts in prophecy, tongues, mystical transports, and healing. A community of individuals whose personal experiences confirmed the experiences of their leaders, actually existed and performed the same indecisive but confirming function for religious experience that the community of persons in art or physical sciences perform for one another. We cannot follow out the various phases in rebuttal of the argument above; it is enough that you understand the procedure: (i) to diminish the overestimate of the certitude of ordinary perception and of the degree to which independent check is decisive and (ii) to indicate the elements present at the origination of the religious tradition which parallel the strengths of the best accredited examples of empirical knowledge.

In matters of religion, as well as in life generally, it seems reasonable "to take his word for it" in cases where it looks to us as if someone else should know what he claims and where our information confirms but does not establish his contentions.

Disclosure and Significance

We can now fulfill our promise in Chapter I to explain how the philosophical arguments for the existence of God may assist the acquisition of faith in God. To do this we introduce the concept "disclosure situation." This enriches our analysis of "significance" by indicating the way in which a new perceptual set may be acquired and the way in which new kinds of experience may arise through readjustments in our assignment of significance to events and appearances. Imagine the following:

An illiterate native is walking along a deserted beach where he discovers a metal object. It glitters in the sun, so he picks it up to examine it. It has a lot of depressable tabs, a round, movable roller and is quite heavy. He puzzles over it and can think of no purpose for it. However, his curiosity compels him to take it home to examine it and to play with it. He bangs its tabs from time to time, eventually noticing that each tab works a steel arm which strikes the soft roller and is accompanied on its release by the roller's moving a little bit to the left. He wonders for a long time over the fact that being hit directly by the metal arm, the roller jumps to the left. Why? How? He also finds that when the roller is all the way over, he can by a special lever push it back and by working the tabs start the jerking movement to the left again. If he never went further in his examination and if his experience remained of a piece with his past, the object might rust away without ever being understood or even seriously wondered at, for wonder itself is a rare commodity among the really primitive. But our native has a spark of genius; he examines the object in greater detail, discovering that there is a curious design on each metal arm and that when you strike hard, the image of the design is cut into the roller. He cannot imagine why anyone would want to do that and notices that after repeated cutting into the roller the images are no longer accurately transferred. This tells him that the images are not supposed to be transferred into the roller, or else that the roller is often to be changed, and he concludes that perhaps the image is to be transferred to something else, something which intervenes. He can think of no purpose such an instrument would serve and abandons his search.

But on a hunting trip he meets a missionary who regales the hunters with stories of Jesus. In the course of the stories, the missionary refers to an object with long lists of little marks which he calls a *Bible*. Our native happens to glance at the thing called a *Bible* and with an excitement like that which accompanied his buying a wife, he recognizes the similarity of the marks to the ones cut into his roller. In a flash it is all clear: he has something you use to make *Bibles*!

He has passed through a disclosure situation. The meaningless has taken on significance.

A disclosure situation is one in which you come upon the way to regard things—a way to regard them whereby the loose pieces fall together: intelligibility is the result of disclosure. From the appreciation of significance, it is only a step to the belief whereby some of the loose ends seem to be accounted for. (You can imagine the hunter's disappointment when he cannot figure out how the large Bible can be placed between the arms and the roller, and should his reasoning be stymied here, the darkness may close about him again; but however dark, it is never again midnight.)

Imagine a student who did not understand the Pythagorean Theorem. His teacher offers a standard proof but there is no answering light in the student's eye. So the teacher resorts to the construction of a right triangle out of quadrille paper and proceeds to cut squares of that paper with sides equal to each of the sides of his triangle. Then he pastes those upon the original figure giving a picture like this:

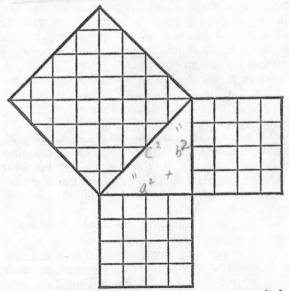

He looks at his pupil but sees no answering light. So he begins to count the little squares within each square-on-a-side. He totals the little squares within A and B and then begins to count the squares in C. Suddenly, as his counting approaches the sum of the squares in A and B, the student exclaims, "Now I see!" The student might not see that what is claimed is true for all right triangles, but he sees what is being claimed; he grasps the import of the theorem. The model-making is a disclosure situation for that student. Examples and illustrations often create disclosure necessary for the communication of abstract ideas.

Now you understand a disclosure situation. It is an experience in which you "get the point" where before you faced the blank and meaningless. Notice that usually you need to be puzzled, to feel your brows knit, before a disclosure is even relevant. There are many kinds of things which create disclosures. Sudden alterings of experience are especially good for this—as Ramsey says, "the penny drops."[19] Disclosures trigger our beliefs about the empirical world. The relatedness of an experience is its significance; the situation in which we come upon the relatedness is the disclosure.

Experience of the horrible, the mysterious, the lovely, the lonely, the evil, the ecstatic, the joyful, the beautiful—all may serve to disclose the relatedness of other experiences and bring one suddenly, or gradually, to a recognition of the presence of God and even to explicit conviction about things to be believed or done.

The New Testament story of the transfiguration seems to be a notable example of a disclosure situation. The vision of Moses and Elias with Jesus took him entirely out of the class of other men, causing the chosen disciples to fall down in fear and wonder. They saw Jesus as someone of great majesty and mystery. A new perceptual set was begun for them. We can actually treat transfiguration as synonymous with disclosure.

Theoretical reasoning can sometimes help. Arguments may assist disclosure. A person may be wondering about the purpose of life. He may read around in the popularizations of religion and philosophy, but cannot "see" the God "stuff"—it means nothing to him because it seems to account for nothing. But then he comes upon a design argument; the argument is urged, embellished with examples, and gradually the way the events of his life are regarded is altered; gradually things take on another significance for him; gradually he experiences the activity of God's intelligence. The argument works here not to create knowledge of its conclusion but to catalyze a state of mind where ordinary experience comes to be regarded as a result of God's acts. "Seeing it that way," the man from what motivation we can only guess, comes to see that it is that way. The argument does not prove this to him; it causes him to see it for himself. This is the midwifery which theoretical considerations may provide to a person of nontheoretical bent. To do this, the arguments need not satisfy the philosopher, they need only work for the person to whom they are given. This is why we said earlier that to assist in religious experience, the intrinsic soundness of an argument is far less important than its apparent soundness.

There is no way *a priori* to say what situations will create disclosure of God or what significance it is appropriate to assign to a given object or event. No object or event has a unique significance; therefore, the perceptual judgments which can be justified by its appearances are never unique. Suppose the native in our example decided to use the object for the creation of ceremonial music in the

---

[19] For a general discussion of the empirical interpretation of religious discourse see Ian T. Ramsey, *Religious Language* (New York, The Macmillan Co., 1957).

form of a rhythmic clicking. Suppose an entire art had developed and had been handed down for centuries. Would it not be true that that was what the object was for? Suppose the tribe were to consider it a divine act by which the object came into its possession, and were to justify that claim by way of the religious function of the object? Could they not be right? Without the native's encounter with the missionary, the "real significance in the object" would perhaps have been quite different.

Moments of disclosure are the great times in the progress of humanity; it is then that man's knowledge takes a forward leap. Is there any reason why human beings may not at their very best see the "speech" of God in the heavens? Not everyone can see this, you say. So, not everyone could see (no matter how we persuade and indoctrinate them) that Bach was a great musician. Not everyone can tell that his automobile starter is defective from the funny clicks he gets where there should have been an energetic start. What you can see depends upon the kinds of experience you can have; that depends upon the significance you assign to the elements of your experience and that depends upon your perceptual sets; and *that* in turn depends very often upon whether you are lucky enough to have met the right disclosure situations. This holds of life generally and is one of the reasons we prize formal university education so highly: the environment is one which creates disclosure situations for the understanding and appreciation of those matters we consider most worthy of man's reflection.

There is no obstacle in principle to the convergence of one's experience to produce the direct perception of God or of God's will. And there is room for reason as well as faith to assist in its acquisition. To understand even the beginnings of the epistemology of religious belief, the student must appreciate the importance of perceptual sets, significance assignments and disclosure situations in the fabric of human knowledge generally.

In this chapter we have set ourselves the modest objective of sketching the relationship between knowledge by faith and knowledge through experience and indicating those features of religious experience and perceptual experience in general which support the following conclusions:

1) "Faith" as applied to matters religious is not some inferior activity incapable of providing knowledge, and substituted where knowledge eludes us. Faith is a species of the most basic human activity in the acquisition of knowledge. We have not explained the relation of "natural faith" to the acquisition of those perceptual sets which dominate our experience. But it should be obvious that our basic interests and ways of regarding things have been *acquired*—acquired through interaction with others and hence, through our trust. The subject needs more detailed explanation than the American and British philosophers have yet given it.

2) The success of one's faith as a means to secure knowledge is dependent upon whether or not the persons at the end of his chain of trust are in a position to know and have taken advantage of it.

3) Where the chain of faith concerns religion, the originators or innovators have usually claimed to have some religious experience. Religious experience as warrant for belief is thus central and fundamental to Western religious tradition.

4) The status of religious experience as warrant for belief is in principle no better or worse than that of any other experience as a warrant for belief—all experience is generated out of the assignment of significance to the data of the senses. It is interesting to ask how the principle will apply to the first items of perceptual knowledge a

child acquires. Of course, after infancy, we never have raw data which are not already assigned some significance before they can arrive from the preconscious into the conscious mind. Further, even the significantly arranged phenomenal data are rarely objects of attention.

5) There is no defect in principle in the knowledge structure which underlies knowledge of God acquired, not through theory, but through teaching and experience.

There is an enormous difference between the attempts of the philosopher and his students to find out for themselves whether God exists, has spoken to man or has promised redemption, and the steps by which the religious believer usually gains his religious belief through teaching, preaching, or religious experience. Moreover, not all religious experience is in the nature of a specific disclosure or perception. Often religious experiences, like other experiences, provide a general reinforcement of the disposition to trust someone's teaching about God.

While there are many basic epistemological questions about the functions of faith and of religious experience yet to be settled, so far no deficiency or deformity has been uncovered which would make religious experience a mutant or deviant of those experiences which function adequately to provide us with empirical knowledge. Any advantage any experience can have has its counterpart in religious experience and any disadvantage that can be indicated in religious experience has its counterpart throughout the whole domain of experience.

CHAPTER III

Evil

INTRODUCTION

FROM AMONG THE THOUSANDS of special subjects discussed by philosophers of religion, we have selected this because of its philosophical interest, its importance to Western religious thought and its affinity to subjects (free will, future contingency, and moral goodness) which form threads throughout the introduction to philosophy.

The subjects of evil, freedom and determinism are closely related because certain theological forms of these problems are generated from common assumptions and the problems are usually given related solutions.

The assumptions which generate the problems of evil—divine foreknowledge and predestination (which theologians have debated for two millennia and which are corollates of the general problems of future contingencies and determinism)—concern both God and man.

It is assumed that God is morally good, benevolent, omniscient, omnipotent, endowed with free choice, acting with providence (a plan which covers all creation) and through government (universal causal control of all events). These characteristics are firmly entrenched in Scripture and tradition. Solutions to our problems which require significant adjustment in or the abandonment of any of these characteristics are to be considered unorthodox. It is further assumed that God stands as final judge of each man, rewarding him with eternal adoption as a son if his life be one of goodness, and with inscrutable justice, condemning the reprobate to an eternity of loss and pain. Over the interpretation of these acts of God a wide latitude is to be found among the orthodox.

It is presumed that man is ignorant (at least in part) of the things which are for his eternal good; that he is inclined by his weakness and ignorance to do evil; that he has free choice and is responsible for his actions, so that when he is eventually judged, he is justly held accountable for righteousness or reprobation. Solutions to the problems we discuss which require abandonment of one of these premises are considered unorthodox (for example, Mather's rejection of free will on the part of man, even though he still tries to preserve man's responsibility for his acts).

Given God's almighty power, goodness and benevolence, how do we account for the presence of so many evils in the world? Given God's power, knowledge, goodness and complete governance, He must forsee and decide whether any given man will be saved and must create each with that knowledge in view; yet how can this be reconciled with the doctrine that the individual man is entirely responsible for his own state before judgment? (a problem of predestination). Moreover, if each man is predestined by God, how can he really have free choice? Is his will not entirely determined through

God's governance? Further, if God knows all things whatever, what He knows must be so and hence occur. So, how can any future event be contingent? Would not the future be necessary? (A problem of future contingency and determinism). And if no man can come to God except by faith and if, when faith results in salvation it does so efficaciously, then how can the will remain free? (a problem of grace and free will). The common assumptions create related problems. The Christian tradition seems based upon the antithesis of human freedom and divine control, and in such a way that, should the tension be reduced by a theory which mitigates either man's or God's power, the result will be unfaithful to the religion.

Because proper sophistication in understanding the various solutions great philosophers have offered is necessary for a worthwhile discussion of these problems, we shall have to concentrate upon the problem of evil, with occasional references to the related questions.

The General Statement of the Problem

There is a very general form of the problem of evil: "Whence the evil in the world?" Given God's goodness, benevolence, power and knowledge, how can we account for the fact that there is evil in the world, both moral and physical? This very general question has other forms: what is the actual rather than the merely possible explanation for the evil of the world? How can we come to know which explanations are even appropriate?

Discussion usually begins in another place and works toward an account of the origin and function of what is evil. The beginnings of the Christians' or Jews' discussion are not in mere wonderment, but in direct confrontation with those who think God does not exist or is not good. From earliest times an attack upon the existence of God and an attack upon the possibility of our knowing that God exists have been based upon the premise that there is evil in the world.

The Direct Challenge Upon the Existence of God

The Epicurean dilemma is illustrative: suppose God exists. Is He willing to prevent evil but not able? Then He is impotent. Is He able, but not willing? Then He is malevolent. Is He both able and willing, then "whence is evil?"[20]

It is assumed that should He be both willing and able to prevent the evils of the world, there would be no evil. This seems reasonable. Hence, if there is evil in the world, there can be no being which is both willing and able to prevent it. But, the argument goes on, if God exists, He is both good and omnipotent; and if God and evil are real, God would have to lack either goodness or almighty power. The evils are real; therefore, God does not exist at all.

Since most persons (who are not philosophers like William James, Tennant, Mill, Brightman, and a host of others who are satisfied with a finite deity) absolutely refuse to consider anything which is finite in power or limited in goodness to be identified with God, that argument constitutes for them a denial of the existence of God.

The student should notice that essential to the Epicurean argument is the assumption that if God is good, He will be willing (He would choose) to remove the evil if He could. It is just this supposition which most theologians have tried to counter,

[20] David Hume, *Dialogues Concerning Natural Religion, Part X*, Haffner Library of Classics (New York, Haffner Publishing Co., 1960).

by means of hypotheses to show that it is quite as possible that God should have had a good reason for permitting the evil. What those rejoinders come to we will see.

The Indirect Challenge to the Existence of God

The elegant David Hume decided to cut the roots of all arguments concerning the existence of God. He excised those based on *a priori* grounds simply by denying that any existence can be necessary. He then tried to knife the jugular of arguments based upon observation of the visible universe.

All arguments for the existence of God which are based upon analogies, for example, between the visible world and artifacts designed by humans would have conclusions which are more or less probable but never absolutely certain. All conclusions based upon observation are probable only. Now if the *antecedent* probability of the conclusion is low enough, such arguments as the design argument will prove nothing. In particular, if it is extremely unlikely, given the structure of the world, that a good and omnipotent God exists, then no observation of the world will ever reveal that a good and omnipotent God does exist. Hume then reasoned that the evil in the visible world renders the hypothesis that a good and omnipotent God exists antecedently improbable. He concludes that no one observing the visible world can reasonably assign a high probability to the existence of God. Hence, one cannot on the basis of his knowledge of the empirical world come to know that God exists. But since Hume has already ruled out *a priori* access to the existence of God and has here ruled out all empirical reasonings to the existence of God, it follows that no reasoning (he allows only *a priori* and empirical reasoning to be possible) will achieve this

conclusion. What cannot in any way be known cannot be reasonably asserted. Hence it is unreasonable to claim to know or even to believe that a good
and omnipotent God exists.

Besides serving to premise the attack upon the
existence of God and upon the possibility of one's
knowing that God exists, the reality of evil has been
used to back up the assertion that the Judaic-Christian conception of God is inconsistent; and hence,
that there is quite satisfactory evidence that certain
of the Judaic-Christian beliefs about God are false.
In particular, either God is not morally perfect or He
is not all-powerful. These are the charges to which
theologians and philosophers have usually directed
their initial replies and from which they have gradually turned attention to the nature of and accounting for evil.

Over and beyond the abstract questions about
the consistency of the conception of God and the
probability that God is morally good, there are existential problems of evil. To these, no theoretical
inquiry provides a resolution. For, while some
theorist may discover a general account of the evil
in the world, he can never account for each and
every particular evil. The events that shake a man's
faith are not the ones explained by a general accounting for evil; they remain the object of our
asking: "Why did this have to happen; God did not
need anything so awful; why did He allow it?" Even
if there be a justification for evils in general, particular evils (when it is you who suffer or when
your eyes are made to look upon the grotesque and
the senseless) are a mystery. Philosophy is no sub-
stitute for faith. It cannot answer the rock-bottom
existential mystery—the individual evil. This is not
surprising because it is merely a correlate of an
even more profound metaphysical problem that
pervades the universe—limitation.

Physical and Moral Evil

It is customary for philosophers to distinguish two classes of evils, the physical and the moral. Not that there has ever been a precise division, or a line clear enough to separate each evil into the class it belongs to. It is only a rough and ready classification which is, perhaps, tidied up when phrased as follows. Moral evil is real in the universe if any intellectual being knowingly does anything that he ought not to have done and does it in the absence of conditions which defeat his voluntariety. Physical evil is real in the universe if some beings have suffered or have been ugly to behold where these situations are caused by nonrational beings, or through actions of rational beings but not acting rationally. Evil is pretty well comprehended in suffering, ugliness, and wrongdoing. Anyone who tries to deny that such things happen and are indeed abundant ignores the facts. Whether these things are really evil in the sense that they ought not to have been permitted to happen at all is another matter.

Conceptions of the Problem

We consider the problem of evil in two forms: as a charge of inconsistency against the Judaic-Christian religion; as a claim that there is a respectable degree of probability that the author of nature (if it be a rational being) cannot be morally good (assuming that it would be almighty). It will turn out that the various classical answers to the second question would, if they were true, provide replies to the very general question: "Whence is evil."

The Incompatibility Charge

Explicit claims that the Judaic-Christian faith is inconsistent because it accepts the "theistic set" (see below) are relatively recent (with, perhaps, the exception of the Epicurean argument). H. J. McCloskey makes the charge explicitly in the first sentence of his paper "God and Evil,"[21] that is: It is inconsistent to hold that God exists, is good, omnipotent, omniscient, provident, governor of the world, capable of free choice and that there is a plentitude of evil (both moral and physical) in the world, which world (with respect to the reality it has) is entirely dependent upon God. This is the so-called "theistic set."

To charge that this body of belief is inconsistent is to claim that it is impossible that all its elements be true, under any possible circumstances. No argument beyond the Epicurean argument has been proposed to support this charge of inconsistency. And that argument cannot work because it insists that if God is both willing and able to prevent evil, we cannot account for the presence of evil. This is true. But who says we must be able to account for the presence of evil? Who says there is an account for the presence of evil? Notice, it is the very person who will try to stop you from arguing, "God exists; for if He does not, we cannot account for the being of anything at all"—that very person will use the same premise to say that the goodness and omnipotence of God leaves us without a way of accounting for the evil of the world, and hence God lacks one or other attribute. He cannot have

21 *The Philosophical Quarterly*, Vol. X, No. 39 (1960), reprinted in *God and Evil*, edited by Nelson Pike (Englewood Cliffs, N.J., Prentice-Hall, Inc., 1964).

it both ways. Either one takes the affirmative or the negative on what must be and what cannot be accounted for. Moreover, as I have already pointed out, the subterranean assumption of the Epicurean argument is that if God were good, God would be willing to prevent the evils of this world. Is that a necessary truth? If so, where is the contradiction inherent in its denial? If it is not a necessary truth, then perhaps it is not true at all! Where is the evidence?

We can do even better than this; we can suggest possible situations in which it would be evident that God's moral perfection would not require His willingness to prevent moral evil. (Thus showing that the principle is not necessarily true.) For instance, suppose that there were some greater good to be achieved through a world with evil in it, a good greater than would be achieved without those evils? Then God's goodness would not require His being willing to prevent the evil. Surely a good being cannot be morally obliged to avoid a greater good than would be otherwise realized! But someone will say: "I can't imagine a greater good to be achieved through the evils conjoined with the other goods than would be achieved by those goods alone." The fact that such is hard to imagine (though if you put your mind to it, you may do so) does not mean that it is impossible to have that happen. If a greater good is not impossible, then it is not necessary that to be good, God must be willing to prevent all evil. This shows you the pattern for dealing with the inconsistency charge. Notice too that if any one of the classical explanations of the origin of evil should actually work, then their mere possibility will have guaranteed the falsity of the conditional "If God is good, He will be willing to prevent all evil."

The Improbability Charge

The chief assumption of the improbability charge is that experience shows us that persons who do not use their power to prevent evil which they could have avoided are morally imperfect. It is argued that God, according to the religious doctrine, had no need whatever to create the universe. So every evil which we observe is one which could have been avoided by means of an alternate creation or through no creation at all. Hence, it is concluded if God did create this universe, He is not morally good.

Moreover, as Hume points out, if one wishes to assemble empirical observations which will lend probability to the hypothesis that the universe is the product of an intelligent and good designer, one should not ignore the evidence to the contrary. Since the evil, both moral and physical, is at least as obvious as the grounds for the design hypothesis, one may not discard it. But taking it into account, one can assign no great probability to the hypothesis that the creator of the world is morally good. In fact, if an agent is to be judged by his work, the designer who produced such an enormity of wrong doing, suffering, and ugliness must be considered more probably defective than excellent.

Hence, even though we may have rejected the charge that the religious doctrines are logically inconsistent, we have here a quite different problem: we are told that it is a fact that if God did create the world with all its evils, God is not morally good. Our arguing to the contrary that He need not have been morally defective in so creating, does not constitute a sufficient rejoinder to the claim that he is in fact morally defective. In addition we are told that the presence of evil in the world is so obvious that we cannot justify an inference, based on the character of the created world, to the moral excellence of the Creator. Rather, the available empirical evidence confirms the contrary.

Traditional Solutions

Augustine: Evil is not truly reality. St. Augustine (c. 400 A.D.) applies the Platonist conception of evil to what was for him a very real existential dilemma.[22] Evil is not being; it is a deprivation, a lack of the excellence in being which belongs there. Since the creator is good, there is no genuine evil in his work, despite the evident pain, ugliness and wrongdoing. (This conception of evil has become an integral part of Western religious and philosophical traditions). Moral evil (which at least approximates genuine evil in that it ought not to occur) is not caused by God but is entirely caused by rational creatures. Human nature is corrupted through vice and habitual wrongdoing; "That it is a nature, this is because it is made by God; but that it falls away from Him, this is because it is made of nothing." He offers a sophisticated psychological analysis of the steps by which a man becomes primarily involved in his own satisfaction and in applying his natural tendency to love almost exclusively to himself, thus destroying in himself the faithful image of God and turning back toward the nothingness from which he came. God cannot be held responsible for what is done freely and responsibly by another. The evils that men do and cause ought not to have happened; but the entire agent of the acts is human.

But what of physical evil, the suffering and evil

[22] St. Augustine, *The City of God*, M. Dodds, trans. Book XIV, 13, 14; pp. 460–462, (New York, Random House, 1950). The attempt to account for the evil in the world pervades all of Augustine's work; his concern stems from his great sensitivity to the workings of man's mind.

not attributed to man? Augustine denies that this
is really evil, really something which ought not to
have happened at all. Whether a given case of suffering or ugliness ought to have been avoided depends upon its utility (For example, to make a dog
suffer while you cure it may not be a cruelty).
He introduces what I call the "tapestry theory." We
cannot, he thinks, from our finite vantage see the
intricate interweaving of the elements of creation
into a magnificent pattern upon which is superim-
posed a sublime coloring of divine redemption.
From God's point of view all suffering and ugliness
is blended into a supreme beauty. We criticize,
judging the tapestry from the knotted threads of its
back. God sees the whole from the front. There can
be no correlation of our earthly judgments with His,
except through faith, through trust in His revela-
tions.

Thus, Augustine's answer boils down to three
claims: (1) there is nothing at all which is strictly
evil in the sense that it ought not to have any reality
at all; (2) some acts of rational creatures ought not
to have occurred—but relatively to their rational
natures and autonomy; (3) other "evils" are only apparently evil.

The difficulties with this answer have seemed to
be enormous right from the beginning. Granted that
moral evil is a privation of the rectitude appropriate to an autonomous creature, and even granting
that God is not responsibile for the acts of rational
creatures, still, God need not have made such creatures. He is responsible for their being. The question then becomes: ought God to have avoided
creating such monsters of iniquity as men so often
are? The "tapestry theory" is again involved: if we
saw the pattern not only of material things, but of
the redemption, and sanctification of the whole
world, the elements would balance into beauty.

Even granted that the overall pattern is more lovely than what would have been attained without these creatures, God's love could have extended to all men the faith which would have been efficacious to their perfection. And besides, what reason can anyone have apart from faith in God (which may be in no way bad for a theologian or a holy person, but which is unacceptable as a premise for the philosopher) by which to conclude that there really is a Providence which draws all the strands into a pattern which reconciles the defects? Again, what effect could God have achieved through this world which He could not have achieved through another which lacks all the evils of this one?

Augustine has simply denied that physical evil falls into the category of what ought not to be realized and has claimed that it is merely in the category of what one of limited knowledge would naturally but incorrectly think ought not to be realized. (But this leaves inexplicable his high praise for the compassion of Jesus in curing men of physical ills). Moral evil is in a relative way what ought not to be realized and, the existence of morally evil agents is analyzed in the same way as the reality of physical evil: all is worked out in the overall tapestry. As an answer to the question "Whence the evil," Augustine offered a speculation which may have some support in faith, but his theory lacks supporting reasons which are available to philosophical scrutiny; and in assigning such great autonomy to rational creatures, Augustine mitigates the universal governance of God.

Spinoza 1632–1677: The ultimate denial of the good-evil distinction. Spinoza, twelve centuries after Augustine, absolutely rejects the tapestry theory, which involves God's achieving an objective which resolves the apparent evils into a greater good. He says, "This doctrine does away with the perfection of God; for if God acts through an object He must desire something which he lacks." He proposed instead that the distinction between good and evil is entirely anthropomorphic—"Everything which conduces to health and the worship of God they have called *good*, everything which hinders these objects they have styled as *bad*." The classification of things as good or bad which stems from human need and desire is entirely relative and in no way reflects the nature of what is real. ". . . the perfection of things is to be reckoned only from their own nature and power; things are not more or less perfect according as they delight or offend human senses, or according as they are serviceable or repugnant to mankind." In Spinoza's opinion, the sufferings of man and his evil acts are not objectively classified. Their only true evaluation is in terms of their imitation of God—and everything satisfies this. Hence, there is no problem of reconciling evil with the goodness of God. From God's point of view whatever is, must be. Hence there can be nothing which objectively ought not to be. Therefore, there is no evil (in the absolute sense of "what ought not to be realized").

The distinction of this view from Augustine's is subtle. There is no evil in the sense of "what ought not to be" for Augustine either, because those things which by themselves (considered as ends in themselves) would rightly be judged as what ought not to be are reconciled in the divine product as a whole and, hence, are given an instrumental justification. With Spinoza there can be no final or distinct project which is really sought by God, and for which things considered evil can be justified as means. Hence, what ought not to be by itself cannot be justified by its incorporation into a greater good. But then, says Spinoza, there can be nothing which ought not to be by itself. For of whatever it is said "it ought not to be" one is speaking relatively to man's desires and tastes and without any relevance to the objective necessity which governs all things. Spinoza's answer has, in fact, denied the freedom of God and the freedom of man, both of which are central to the religious tradition. His theory constitutes an extreme application of the Augustinian denial that there is any genuine evil.

The remaining reconciliations of the goodness of God with the evil in the world fall into two groups: those which say God could not have avoided the evil; and those who say God need not have avoided it.

Theories: *That God could not have avoided evil.* These theories do not attempt to deny that there are some evils, some things which "ought not to have been" from the point of view of humans; but they say that given the objective of God to create a world of free and intelligent beings, they could not have been avoided and hence, have no objective status as things which ought not to have been. There is no status as what ought not to be which must be justified by inclusion in some extraneous end, as St. Augustine thought.

Leibniz (1646–1716) took an extreme view which is supposed to fit into the crevice between the views of Spinoza and Augustine. This is the best of all possible worlds, but not the only one. God in His perfection would not have made less than the best among the choices open to Him. His governing necessity is not natural but moral—He was morally required to create the world because of its intrinsic merits. Thus in an absolute sense of what ought not to be there is nothing in this world which is evil, though God's having created such things is not excluded by His nature. All those things which, when considered by themselves and

apart from their place in the best possible world
might be considered "what ought not to be" are
denied that status by their position as elements in
the best of all possible worlds. He concedes to
Spinoza that there is no pattern of greater good to
be achieved, no object or end to which creation is
directed: it is created because of its intrinsic merits.
He concedes to Augustine and Spinoza that there
really is nothing which objectively "ought not to be"
and yet he preserves God's free choice against
Spinoza by insisting that He was motivated by what
is best to be rather than what must be. What God
cannot (in His moral perfection) avoid cannot be
absolutely evil (something which He ought to have
avoided). There can be evil only insofar as the
created will ought not to do certain things or insofar
as the created being finds something unpleasant
(physical evil). The whole of Leibniz' *Theodicy* is
devoted to the project of explaining and defending
this doctrine. The chief strength of the doctrine lies
in the "best possible world" hypothesis. If this world
is required by God's perfection, then no part of it can
constitute evidence that He is imperfect.

The chief weakness of the theory lies also in the
supposition there could be a best of all possible
worlds. From God's point of view (as God is tradi-
tionally conceived), He is infinitely imitable and any
state of being which imitates God is, so far, good.
There is no finite imitation of God which could
not be surpassed. Because all creations will be finite, there cannot be a best possible world. Notice,
the sense in which God could not have avoided
evil in Leibniz' theory is not the sense of "it is
logically impossible that" simply and by itself. It is
that it is logically impossible, *given* that this is the
best possible world and that God is morally determined to seek the best, which, therefore, can have
no element He ought to have avoided. The argu-

ment is entirely *a priori* and its defect lies in the inherent inconsistency of the "best possible world" hypothesis.

Other forms of the doctrine that God cannot be found morally imperfect because He could not have avoided the evils of the world are these. The laws of nature and the laws of free beings could not be as they are without the occurrence of some evil. Some good would be impossible without some moral evil (for example, the virtue of "fortitude" would be impossible without some injustices). A perfect world is not possible without the variety which would allow some evil.

But the defect of these proposals is obvious. They miss the point. The "necessity" is merely hypothetical. Even granting that the evils are built into the laws of the world, the universe as such was avoidable by God; hence, its evils could have been avoided.

To argue that the evils are justified by the good they occasion is to make entirely unsupported assumptions about the balance of goods and evils[23] and also to assume that the goods occasioned by these evils could not have been replaced or surpassed by goods not occasioned by evil. Even if the assumptions were true, they would not assure us that God could not have avoided the evils without diminution of His moral excellence. St. Thomas Aquinas (who offered the first two arguments and tried, at one time or another, almost every answer to the problem of evil) also presents the further argument[24] that a perfect world is not possible without the variety

[23] See St. Thomas Aquinas, *Summa Contra Gentiles*, III, 71, No. 6; translated into English and in paperback under title *The Truth of the Catholic Faith*. Image Books (New York, Doubleday & Co. Inc., 1956).

[24] St. Thomas Aquinas, *Summa Contra Gentiles*, III, 71, No. 3.

which includes evil. But what reason is there to think that this is a perfect world, unless we already beg the question by assuming this to be the perfect product of a perfect artist? To say that God absolutely could not have avoided the evils seems inconsistent with traditional doctrine; to make the "could not" merely conditional is to adopt one of the following kinds of theory.

That God need not have avoided evil. There are two sorts of reasons given for this claim: a) that such a creation is at least permissible; b) that God ought to have made things as they are.

To show that such a creation is permissible, it is sometimes argued:

(1) The greater good on the whole results in such a world.

(2) The evils of the world are admonishments to man.

(3) The evil that results from defects in the secondary causes cannot be imputed to God.

The first is another version of the tapestry theory, since no one is willing to say just what greater good is achieved by the world. We need not argue that this theory is impossible; it is not. But to serve as an answer to the charges that God in fact ought to have avoided the evils of the world, the mere possibility of this hypothesis is not sufficient. We must have some reason for thinking it true. We have none which would not already suppose the goodness of God. If we had a good and independent reason to think (1) is true, we would have an acceptable answer to the improbability charge. But we have no such reason, at least none which is epistemically independent of the religious tradition which is at stake.

The second principle is plainly false. Moreover, what needs demonstration is that man ought to take the evils in the world as warnings rather than as evidence against the justice of God since the evil seems to be laid upon the saints even more heavily than upon the sinners.

The third principle expresses the main thrust of all Aquinas' reasoning and of all the reasoning of the other great theologians, too. The evils, both physical and moral, result from defects in secondary causes and not in God, the primary cause. But such writers do not explain why, if we account for the effects (which are evils) by postulating the defects of the secondary causes, we should not go on to account for their defects by postulating defects in the primary cause, God. This is the whole question at issue. As we said earlier Hume assumes that if God is benevolent and good He must be willing to avoid the evils. St. Thomas and others think He need not be so willing, because the evils result from defects in created causes. But we can, in the spirit of Hume, ask why God was not willing to avoid defects in the secondary causes or avoid creating them at all. Why is God not responsible for their defects? Why is it that sometimes we may infer from a defective effect (a particular physical or moral evil) to a defect in its cause (the created natural cause or the created human agent) and that at other times we may not do so (e.g., infer a defect in a primary cause because of the defect in its product)? This is the really crucial point. If a satisfactory answer is to be given, it will follow that God cannot be blamed for the evil in the world and Hume's attack will have been parried. (Though not his charge that we cannot *infer* the goodness of God from the character of creation.)

It is sometimes argued that God ought not to avoid the evils we observe because:

(1) They are the punishments for moral evil which God need not have prevented.

(2) They are the natural consequences (but not necessarily punishments) for moral evil.

It is premised that God need not have prevented moral evil because this would require His interference with the natural behavior of things.[25] But of course it would not. For one way to have prevented moral evil would have been to create no such being; that involves no interference. Moreover, what evidence is there that physical evil is our punishment for moral evil? Children would then be punished for the sins of their fathers and the innocent for the crimes of fiends. The distribution of evils would require, if they were punishments, that God be so consistently unjust that He could not possibly be morally good. The punishment hypothesis defeats the very proposition that God is good which it was supposed to save.

The hypothesis that physical evil is a natural consequence for the moral evil but not a separately imposed punishment requires that all evil results from a wrongdoing of rational creatures (not necessarily men) and that apart from such wrongdoing there would have been no ugliness or suffering in the universe. This is not utterly implausible, but it is ineffective because it requires us to ask why God does not avoid the moral evils of rational creatures? If we are told again that avoiding the evils would have required divine interference with the behavior of free creatures, we can again reply effectively that: not to have created rational creatures would have involved no interference; and to have aided the will of each rational creature with efficacious supernatural grace (as thought by some to have happened to the mother of Jesus) in such a way as to preserve the creature from all evil, is

---

[25] St. Thomas Aquinas, *Summa Contra Gentiles*, III, 71, No. 45.

possible (according to the religious tradition) without interfering with the freedom of the will.

Hence, God had at least two ways in which to avoid the evils without interfering with the freedom of its creatures. So, unless there is some greater good or some higher purpose to be achieved through such a creation, the hypothesis that physical evil is a natural consequence of moral evil is of no explanatory value. Yet, if we assume that we can justify God's failure to avoid moral evil in the world, then on the hypothesis that physical evil results naturally from moral evil, we can justify the presence of physical evil, too.

None of these answers to the charge "If God is able but not willing to avoid the evils of the world, He must not be good" is decisive or even persuasive. To say this need not have been true because it is logically possible that a greater good justify the evil is not to answer the charge that it is in fact true, even though it need not have been; (but it at least defeats a decisive inference from the evils of the world to the imperfection of God). To say God could not have avoided the evils must either commit us to a limited power on God's part or to the existence of an objective for creation, which we can only postulate but never prove to exist. For we know that Leibniz is wrong to consider this the best possible world, as was Spinoza to consider it the only possible one. Since the religious context commits us to God's omnipotence (though a significant number of philosophers have become unorthodox on this point),[26] we have open only the "postulated objective" hypothesis, and this fails to

[26] John Stuart Mill in *Three Essays on Religion*, 1884 says we must recognize God's power to be limited. So too, William James. This was a common nineteenth century idea which paved the way for the "Process God" of Whitehead.

provide an answer just because it is *ad hoc.* The objective is postulated only in order to reconcile the putative goodness of God with the reality of evil. The "greater good" objective need be postulated only on the hypothesis that God is good; but from its being postulated, the goodness of God need not follow logically, and the very procedure of postulating it can be said to beg the question about whether God is good. We have no independent reason to hold that there is some higher good which is achieved. Therefore, we cannot use the hypothesis in answer to the improbability challenge, although we can employ it to defeat the inconsistency charge.

Attempts to argue that God need not have avoided evil (that is, to argue that being unwilling to avoid evil is not the same as being malevolent or evil) are interesting but are unsupported at crucial points. That there is a greater good to be achieved in which the evils are reconciled is what needs to be demonstrated. That evils which result from defects in secondary causes cannot be imputed to the primary cause, is just what needs to be proved. Showing either of these things would establish the falsity of the assumption that if God is unwilling to avoid the evils of our world, He is morally imperfect (it being granted that God is fully able to avoid the evils). This is all that is needed to defend the goodness of God against Hume's suggestion that nature evidences God's imperfection as much as His goodness. None of the traditional answers goes significantly further than we have indicated and none, therefore, supplies what is needed. Now I shall make a few suggestions about new directions, suggestions which indicate that the imperfection of God cannot be evidenced in nature but not that His goodness can be demonstrated from observation of His work.

But first, ask yourself this: Is it logically possible that there should be a world which it would be evil for God to create? If God cannot do evil and if God is all-powerful, then no possible world is such that it would be evil for God to create. If that is so, then God can create a world in which, as time passes, more and more beings suffer pain and do evil until no finite being loves God and all are tortured, utterly corrupt, and surrounded by ugliness. Is not such a world consistent? Then it is possible. Then God can create it. Therefore there is no connection between the degree of depravity, pain, and ugliness in the created world and God's moral qualities, if God is morally perfect. But why is the distribution of evil in the world irrelevant to the moral qualities of God? Why can we not impute the defects of the things in the world to their maker?

If we succeed in providing a reason for this, we shall have disposed of the contention that God is not good if He, though able, is unwilling to remove the evil from our world. But we shall have done so at the expense of granting the second point Hume makes: that from a study of creation you cannot inductively conclude to the goodness of God. Suppose that is so, then how can a person come to know that God is good? I leave this question for your consideration after we settle its preliminaries.

Refutation of the Case against the Goodness of God. Consider this rule of limited inference:[27]

If A and B are entities of different levels of reality such that A is of higher level than B, no inference

---

[27] The remaining arguments of this chapter, the rule of limited inference, and the definition of difference of reality levels are the same, as far as space permits, as the somewhat more elaborate treatment I have given to this problem in *Philosophical Theology*, Chapter VI, especially in Section 5, pp. 250–272.

from the fact that B has a property F to the conclusion that A has the property F is warranted unless it is logically impossible that Fb, if it be false that Fa; or unless there is inductive grounds that if Fb then Fa, where the induction is based upon instances of pairs of things related by the same difference in level of reality.

This rule is plain common sense, as you will see if you consider the weird inferences that would become justified on the supposition that it is false.

Thus, it is unwarranted to infer from the fact that the characters in a play like swordplay to the conclusion that the author does, or from the fact that most of your dream beings are beautiful, to the fact that you are. Yet it is not unreasonable to say that if your dream figures are always embroiled in problems, there is some probability that you are, too. For in this case, we have wide enough acquaintance with the properties of beings of both levels to set up some inductive correlations. This is also the case in some respects between authors and the characters in their literary output.

Different Levels of Reality. Since you may be puzzled by the expression different levels of reality, let us define it, acknowledging that with respect to its definition there are borderline cases which are not easily resolved, but insisting that according to certain notions widespread in the history of philosophy concerning the relationship of man to God and of man to his own quasi-creatures of thought and will (and of a substance to the quality which modifies it), such a relationship has always been supposed to obtain.

Because saying that two beings are of different levels of reality means that one of the entities is of a lower level of reality than the other, we shall define that expression.

B is of a lower level of reality than A if and only

if: B belongs, in virtue of what sort of thing it is, to
a class of things such that no member of that class
could exist unless: (1) some member of the class of
things to which A belongs, in virtue of what sort of
things it is, actually exists; (2) actually produces the
existing members of B's class; and (3) maintains a
conserving relationship to those members throughout their existence; (4) and no member of B's class
has any property whatever that is not bestowed
upon it by some member of A's class or some member of some class of things to which the members
of A's class stand in relations (1), (2) and (3).

As given, this definition has some defects; but
the symbolism required to avoid them is too complex for beginning students and the loss of clarity
involved in a technically accurate definition is self-
defeating.

This definition does not preclude an infinite set
of levels of reality; nor is there any reason to think
there can be no such set. The relation which a particular thing of lower level has to the particular thing
of higher level which produces it is called metaphysical dependence. All of the members of the
higher class are said to be ontologically prior to
those of the lower. Metaphysical dependence is a
relation which obtains between particular effects
and their causes where the effects are of a lower
level of reality than their causes.

This is not a relation of simple causal dependence,
since particular effects can perdure when all members of the class to which their cause belonged have
ceased to exist. Neither is this a relation of simple
logical dependence. Reality level difference requires
the logical dependence of the classes (as well as
the individuals) so that the lower cannot have members if the other does not (but not vice versa).
Thus, it is possible that some mind might exist although no imaginary being exists. Yet there cannot

exist an imaginary being unless some mind exists and imagines. The principle that no finite being could exist if an infinite being did not, is not debated here; it is accepted as within the data of the problem.

An examination of the fundamental forms of argument against God's righteousness and power and against His determining providence[28] shows that the arguments make one of two mistakes: either they supposed that things which are by nature of different levels of reality are not (and therefore ignore essential attributes of God); or they presuppose as a premise, connecting the facts of free will or evil with the powers and attributes of God, a general proposition which is false or one which epistemically inaccessible. This causes the arguments to violate the rule of limited inference.

The reason why these mistakes have eluded theologians and philosophers is that the *prima facie* case against God's goodness presupposes an analogy which is incorrect but quite natural.

The analogy in question is that propositions, which apparently hold of relations between men and other men or physical entities and other physical entities, also hold of God. Thus, just as a man who *makes* another man kill a third is responsible and, perhaps, morally deficient and, in any case, destroys the free will of the second man's act, so also with God who does the same, not merely by command but by causal power, with respect to a creature. Again, a man who causes needless suffering which he could morally have avoided and could have avoided without cost must lack moral perfection. So also with God. These presupposed analogies are at least psychologically the traducers of philosoph-

---

[28] Whether they consciously employed it or not is not in question; that they needed it is claimed.

ical thought on the problem we are considering and their fallaciousness is established, I think, by what follows.

The Argument against Free Will. (a) Since Judaic-Christian doctrine holds quite definitely that "God wills that p" (where p is contingent) is a necessary and sufficient condition that *p* (because nothing can occur which God has not willed to occur, and whatever God wills to occur, occurs), it has been argued that man cannot be free.

(b) If a man, A is free to do *x*, then for any act *x* which A does freely, "A wills to do *x*" is a sufficient condition for "*x* occurs" (all other things being equal), and nothing else is actually a sufficient condition for A's doing *x*.

Either it is incompatible with the description (b) to say that God's choice is a sufficient condition of my doing what I do, or there are disparate kinds of sufficiency or causality (as we know well that philosophers have long supposed: see Aristotle, Plato, Aquinas, and Berkeley with whom the matter is clearest in the distinction between the kind of causal dependence among ideas and the kind of dependency between minds and ideas.)

If one rests his argument against God's determining providence upon supposing an incompatibility between God's being a sufficient cause of the free act and the creature's also being its sufficient cause, then he treats God and creatures as being of the same level of reality. For one should note about beings of different levels of reality that natural causal sufficiency can obtain only among beings of the same level while at the same time with regard to a being of higher level, metaphysical casual sufficiency can also obtain. Consider the fact that Macbeth is the sufficient natural cause of Duncan's death, while at the same time Shakespeare is the sufficient cause both of Macbeth's doing what he did and of its having that effect. To treat man and God as of the same level of reality is to ignore a basic element in the idea of God, that man could not have existed had God not chosen to create him. It is to make an error as silly as it would be to confuse the activity of Macbeth with that of Shakespeare. Thus we can dismiss this sort of argument against God's providence because it contradicts the data of the problem.

But if the case is not rested upon this premise, to what must one appeal in order to establish the incompatibility of God's sufficiency and man's sufficiency for the same event? He must appeal to something like the following statement: R1: That for anything A, which acts freely, it is false that A is metaphysically dependent upon something else. (For, by the definition of that relation, A is of lower level of reality than something else and has a sufficient cause of all its characteristics, including the fact that it performs the act in question from some higher being).

If this is not presupposed, then there is no logical connection between the two claims: "God's willing so is the sufficient cause for A's doing y" and "A's willing to do y is the sufficient cause for A's doing y." Inference that the one excludes the other violates the rule of limited inference. But the principle must not be presupposed, either, because it is demonstrably false.

If it were true, it would be impossible for any being, including God, to create a free being. But the Shakespeare-Macbeth relation, and the author-character relation in general, fulfill the conditions for reality level difference and of metaphysical dependence, (as we defined it). They stand as a counterexample to the principle. There is no reason, therefore, to infer from the fact that creatures are free that God does not determine their actions, since there is no logical connection between the two claims. Hence, the argument against God's determining causality violates the rule of limited inference.

It is to be noted that the argument here is not by analogy from the author-character relation to the creator-creature relation, but is rather a deduction from a relation (metaphysical dependence) of which both are equally instances.

The Question of Evil. For every cause of a physical evil (suffering, ugliness, etc.) which is on the same level of reality as the thing which suffers the evil (and is, therefore, its natural cause), there is a higher-level sufficient cause which brought it about that the lower-level suffering occurred; this is elementary religious doctrine. The higher-level thing, God, could have avoided the occurrence of the physical evil by alterations in what exists or in the causal laws governing what exists. But to argue that there is a moral defect in the higher-level cause because it does not preclude the evil is to presuppose as warrant for such a conclusion a proposition which is false.

Suppose we have the following premise: (1) God, of higher level of reality than creatures, could have precluded all sufferings in His creatures.

How do we get to the conclusion that God ought to have done so? By means of a second premise:

(2) Any being which could avoid or preclude the sufferings of others without a moral defect in the act of precluding ought to do so. This looks plausible until we see that it commits us to this statement—Any being which could without a moral defect preclude the sufferings of other beings on a lower level of reality, or in beings which are metaphysically dependent upon it ought to do so.

This more specific premise is needed because God cannot be on the same level of reality as His crea-

tures if the Christian doctrine of creation is true.
By the same arguments with regard to sufficiency
Shakespeare cannot be on the level of reality ten-
anted by his characters. But we know that it is
false that Shakespeare ought to have prevented the
death of Desdemona. Hence, the general principle
(R2) is false. Therefore, any inference which employs it as the justifying connection for passing from
premise to conclusion is unsound.

More than all this, the premise (2) is false (as is
easily seen) when restricted to creatures of the
same level and on that ground alone ought not to
be employed as a proof of the more specific premise. But even if it were true, it would be a patent
equivocation on the term "preclude" to say R2
follows from (2), since in (2) we are speaking of
precluding by natural causality and in R2 we are
speaking of precluding by metaphysical causality.

Moral Evil. If Jones sins in murdering Smith, then
Jones must have been the sufficient cause of what
was done, otherwise he is not the responsible agent.
But if Jones sins in murdering Smith, it is also
true that God willed that Jones sins in murdering
Smith and that God's will is sufficient for its occurring that Jones sins in that act. Is every sufficient
cause of a morally evil act morally responsible for
that evil? Obviously not. For if Jones sins in murdering Smith, why should we say that God is defective bringing this about? By an additional principle that whenever A causes B to sin in doing *x*,
A sins also? But this is an obvious equivocation on
"cause." For, ordinarily if A causes B to do *x* (which
would normally be a sin for B) the fact that A
causes B to do *x* exonerates B from the charge of
having sinned. This implies that God can be responsible for the morally evil acts of his creatures only
on the condition that they are not morally reprehensible! That is equivalent to saying that God is

morally defective for creating a world with morally evil creatures only if He did not do so.

Yet God did create a world in which there is moral evil, where beings with full knowledge that what they are doing ought not to be done, freely act and are morally reprehensible. Hence it follows that God is not to be blamed for the moral evil in the world as long as the principle is maintained that if there is a sufficient cause distinct from B of B's doing the evil act, then B is not responsible.

But it will be pointed out that where beings are of different levels of reality, that principle cannot apply because the term "cause" becomes equivocal, just as we pointed out above.

In that case the argument that God is morally defective requires a new premise R3: When a being of higher level is sufficient cause of the free evil action of a being of lower level, the higher being is morally defective and ought not to have caused that act.

This principle is shown to be false by the same sort of examples which were given above. Moreover, when one seeks reasons to support this principle, its absurdity becomes palpable. Therefore, the inference from the existence of morally defective creatures to a moral defect in God is unsound.

Because applying a particular form (applicable only to God's relationships to creatures) of R1, R2, or R3 as a premise to validate these inferences would beg the question which the argument is designed to settle, the universal form alone can be employed. Yet the universal forms of the premises considered are all false. Hence, the arguments are unsound. Let me explain further.

The talk about the relations of mental beings to minds which conceive them and of fictional or imaginary beings to their authors might lead you to think I am drawing an analogy between these states of affairs and the relationship of God to the world. This is not true and is not the point of the argument. Rather, I am showing that there are only two sorts of principles about the moral relationships between beings of higher level and their metaphysical effects which could validly connect the proposition "God is good, creator, omnipotent, etc." with the proposition "there is evil and suffering in the world" in such a way as to yield the conclusion that God is morally defective. The first sort is a general proposition of the forms R_1, R_2, or R_3, given above. Each is clearly false because the author-character and dreamer-dream cases are counterexamples. The other sort of principle, which would concern only metaphysical causes with real beings as effects (the proposition R' discussed below) will beg the question. Thus, the point of the discussion of metaphysical causality is to get a fundamental element of God's relation to the world made clear so that it will be evident that these two sets of principles, (R_1, R_2, R_3 and R'), are the only sorts that will make the usual inference against the goodness of God valid. To ignore the reality level difference merely causes equivocation. Now, we have rejected R_1 and R_2 and R_3 as plainly false. Let us see what happens to R'. If, as I contend, it begs the question, then the argument against the goodness of God, though valid where R' connects the main premise to the conclusion, is not and cannot be made successful.

It might be said that the principle R_2 may be true when restricted to actual or real beings. Now why this restriction, I do not see (beyond its apparent value as an *ad hoc* escape from the argument) since all the cases I have given fit the definition of metaphysical dependence. But I will grant the restriction. Thus we get a principle P: "Any being which could without cost or moral defect preclude or avoid the evil acts and sufferings of other real beings and fails to do so is morally imperfect."

But this principle, which is confirmed by our moral experience or at least by our moral ideals, does not entail R′, the principle needed. R′: "Any real being which could without cost or moral defect avoid or preclude the evil acts and sufferings of real beings which are metaphysically dependent upon it and fails to do so is morally imperfect."

For to say R′ follows from P is to equivocate on the concepts of cause which are involved in "preclude" and "avoid." There are two kinds of precluding or avoiding. Our evidence for P is based upon experiences which involve natural causality. How can we without further reason shift to a principle involving metaphysical causality, especially when cases were given in which the stronger rule R2 did not hold (where the dependent beings were not restricted to real beings)?

The theist must grant, as the nontheist does, that God could have avoided the evils in the world without moral defect and without cost. For the theist must hold that there is no end which God in any way needs for His happiness, pleasure or moral perfection which can be provided only by creation. (God did not need to create. Hence, no cost and no imperfection if no creation at all.) The theist must also grant that God failed to avoid or preclude these evils.

The nontheist needs R′ to make his case. For if R′ is false, nothing follows from the fact that God created a world with evils He could have avoided, which would supply any reason for our believing that God is morally imperfect. If it cannot be established that R′ is true, there is no case against God's goodness to be answered.

The establishing of R′ as a premise cannot succeed. For (a) R′ begs the question and, (b) R′ cannot be known to be true; R′ is epistemically inaccessable.

R′ begs the question.

(1) There is only one possible substitution instance for the first occurrence of "real being" in R′ since God alone can create other beings which are real.

(2) Hence, R′ is equivalent to A: If God could, and fails to, avoid the evil acts and sufferings of real beings metaphysically dependent upon Him when He could do so without cost or moral defect, God is morally imperfect.

(3) Now both theist and atheist must grant the antecedent: that God could have avoided all evil and suffering of real beings without cost or moral defect.

The nontheist wants to grant this to urge his opponent into the consequent; the theist, because he holds that no creation is necessary for God's beatitude. Hence, no creature could be avoided only at a cost to God.

(4) The theist thus sees the whole matter as an issue of denying the inference, A, which he takes the nontheist to be bent upon establishing.

(5) But the nontheist's principle R′ used to establish this inference, A, is nothing but a restatement of A. Hence to insist that R′ is the premise his case employs is merely to beg the whole question of whether God is morally perfect, unless the nontheist will go on to show that it is true.

But R′ cannot be shown to be true, cannot be established by philosophical analysis. Only two avenues are open: to show that R′ is necessary (and therefore true) or to show that R′ follows from premises we know to be true or to show that some experience confirms it.

I cannot imagine a proof of the necessity of R′,

since it is possible (i.e., logically consistent) that although God could have eliminated the evils without cost there might be some balance of good and evil which would justify the evils, just as several others of the twelve "Reconciliations" of divine goodness and evil in the world are possible (i.e., consistent).

There cannot be a proof of the truth of R′ from things we know to be true. For R′ does not follow from P and other truths about the relationships of natural agents, (agents of the same level of reality). For any proposition K from which R′ follows, it will be quite evident that K is no more surely a matter of knowledge than R′, which is now in doubt since our knowledge of metaphysical dependence is limited indeed and easily surveyed.

There cannot be a proof of the truth of R′ from experience. For if R′ is not revealed truth, what experience other than a divine revelation would tell us it is true? And if it were said to be divinely revealed, it would, in combination with the observed evil in the world, convict God of moral defect; so then we would have good reason to doubt the truth of the revelation, since God's veracity will go the way of God's morality.

If it were said that R′ needs no proof, that we all know it to be true, that assertion would be simply false.

Since it cannot be shown that there is or could be any reason to accept R′ either from logic or from experience or from whatever else we know, it is indeed unjustifiable for a philosopher to employ R′ as a premise to attack the goodness of God. It just begs the question.

As a result, there is not and cannot be a case against either the moral perfection of God or against the all-pervasive determining will of God based upon our observations of the evil in the world.

Does this mean that the moral character of God cannot be established through knowledge gained from the structure of the world, as Hume contended? Yes, it does mean that. Yet I do not deny that observing the world, one may find many things to rejoice in and admire God for. Nor do I deny that an understanding of the world in the light of the economy of salvation may disclose that even the sufferings of men and their being doomed to death and dissolution fit into a plan wholly admirable. Nor do I deny that the goodness of God can be discovered from the structure of the world (as was sketched in Chapter 2); I merely deny Hume's claim that the imperfection of God is the more probable hypothesis warranted by our experience.

CHAPTER IV

Cognitivity and Analogy

FOR AS MANY CENTURIES as philosophers have debated the truth of particular statements about God, they have also debated whether religious beliefs (e.g., "God loves us," "God redeemed the world," "All men can enter into divine life") are cognitively meaningful and cognitively accessible.

Since philosophers often leave questions about meaningfulness entangled with questions about truth, their disputes are more confusing and inconclusive than they need be. This is the more evident when questions of the form—"Is it meaningful, more than emotively or performatively?" are confused with questions of the form "How do we find out that it is true or is not," or when either of these is confused with those of the form "Is it true?"

It is one thing to examine the structure of the human knowing process in order to find the evidence patterns according to which religious claims can be assessed as true or false—this is what we already sketched in Chapter 2—it is quite another to apply some criterion of meaning to discourse in order to crank out a decision as to the cognitive meaningfulness of religious assertions. It is still a third (and much more important) thing to provide a generally adequate analysis of or theory about the way we actually extend meaningful discourse from circumstances where direct observation is possible, to circumstances where normal sense-experience no longer applies. In the first instance, we are applying general epistemological considerations to the area of religion. In the second, we are applying a criterion of meaningfulness to religious discourse. In the third, we are constructing a partial theory of language which may account for the meaningfulness of religious discourse: that is the purpose of the analogy theory.

COGNITIVITY

The religious beliefs of Christianity are, at least in principle, cognitively *accessible* through the chain of teaching which originates (according to religion itself) in the direct experiences of prophets and apostles. If the conditions supposed by the religion are true, the believers have knowledge, and not merely true belief in what it teaches. (This can be established by means of a more general analysis of testimonial evidence than we have provided in the second chapter of the text.) If the conditions presupposed are not fulfilled, the teachings of Christianity are still cognitively accessible in principle, though they may be false. (You must remember that even false propositions are cognitively accessible—otherwise we can't find out that they are false.) It is therefore pointless for one to say that the teachings of Christianity are in principle inaccessible to human knowledge. That would be equivalent to insisting that testimony cannot for

us be a means of acquiring knowledge or false belief about God.

Still, one outcome of a cognitive assessment of
another's utterance is that it is meaningless. That
is, we can say of another's utterance that it is false,
true, meaningless, contradictory, pointless, etc.; but
the outcomes relevant here are: true, false, or
meaningless. Testimony and examination will disclose the truth or falsity of religious belief only if
what is believed is meaningful. A fair number of
philosophers and theologians have seriously argued
that the characteristic claims of Christianity are
cognitively meaningless, that is, that they have no
content which is appropriate for belief or disbe-
lief. To say that something is meaningless in this context is not merely to say that it is without meaning
for someone in particular, but rather that it is without meaning for anyone at all. Such a verdict could
be supported for the whole class of Christian religious beliefs only by some argument based upon
a general criterion of meaningfulness which is applicable to all statements regardless of their subject
matter. This is exactly what was attempted by the
logical positivists who developed the strong and
weak empirical verification criteria. Unfortunately,
theologians were in large numbers frightened by
the apparent danger to religion from the positivist's conclusion that metaphysical and religious
statements are empirically meaningless because they
cannot be empirically verified, and began a large-
scale retreat into other accounts of religious meaning (emotive and other noncognitive accounts) before it was widely recognized by philosophers that
there is no generally acceptable criterion of empirical meaning, much less of cognitive meaning in
its widest sense.

A student who would enjoy tracing the various

steps in the positivist attack and the theologian's feints and countermoves will find W. T. Blackstone's *The Problem of Religious Knowledge* (Prentice-Hall, Inc., 1963) or Frederick Ferré's *Language, Logic and God* (Harper & Row, 1961) useful. It will be readily apparent that the positivist attacks overshot the mark and that the theologians' replies are, none of them, systematically convincing. In the light of what we know now, the debate was as archaic as a fencing duel during an atomic war.

The noncognitivist and verificationist theories of the theologians do not get at the heart of the difficulties and do not accord proper weight to certain obvious facts, the most important of which is the fact that these Judaic-Christian beliefs are formulated in ordinary language and that there is not the slightest antecedent reason to believe that ordinary words are misused in the statement of such beliefs. Noncognitivist accounts of religious meaning are like a coroner's report upon a man who hasn't had an accident yet.

The epistemological investigation of Chapter II of this text presupposed that the characteristic religious teachings of Christianity have specific and definite cognitive content. For example, the teaching that Jesus was a man is assumed to claim that Jesus was really and not merely apparently a man. Thus, even though the religious teaching that Jesus was a man is itself neutral (even indeterminate) to a large number of theoretical translations (e.g., "Jesus was an individual animal-rational substance"—an Aristotelian view, or "Jesus was an embodied divine soul" —a neo-Platonic view), it is not neutral to (or compatible with) all theoretical interpretations and is not compatible with every purported ordinary language paraphrase. Ordinary religious belief-statements are indeterminate with respect to a large number of theoretical formulations which impose precision upon them. But they do have enough content to restrict the range of such interpretations.

The characteristic religious teachings of Christianity are things every Christian will admit can be misunderstood, misinterpreted, and can be disputed (both as to correct interpretation and as to truth). Given that these things are true, it would be a simple misconstruction of the problems of religious discourse for us to leave it an open option to say that the characteristic teachings of Christianity are cognitively vacuous. That the religious beliefs may be conjunctively false is logically possible; that they are cognitively vacuous is absurd. If we will accept certain kinds of linguistic behavior among groups of persons as definitive evidence that their utterances have cognitive content, then we shall find that any linguistic practices (x, y, z) which in a nonreligious context (C) provide us sufficient evidence for the cognitivity of nonreligious utterances in C, have empirically established analogues (x', y', z') in religious contexts which will serve the same function—namely, to establish the cognitivity of the religious utterances. The standard countermove to this argument is to cite some principle of cognitive meaningfulness which the utterances in C satisfy and which the religious utterances will fail to satisfy— e.g., the verifiability or falsifiability criteria of meaning. But since no criterion of meaningfulness has been found to be generally applicable, in a nonreligious or even purely scientific context, this sort of counterattack is not to be taken seriously. Hence, we can rest our claim for the cognitivity of traditional Christian belief upon the obvious similarities between religious discourse and discourse of other sorts and also upon the appropriateness of the kind of investigation into the nature of testimony and its experiential and evidential origins which we outlined in Chapter II. That sort of investigation would be inappropriate, were the testimony in question cognitively vacuous. There can be no evidence of testimony where the witnesses merely express their feelings, evoke yours, or mumble vacuities.

We do not need an analogy theory, then, to answer whether or not Christian religious teachings are cognitively meaningful. It is already evident that the religious teachings are cognitively (rather than merely emotionally) meaningful. Rather, an analogy theory will supply an account (an explanation of how meaning is transferred from directly empirical contexts to nonempirical contexts) of the cognitivity of the religious discourse. The analogy theory will not help to show whether the beliefs are true or false; but it will dispel the miasmic and paralytic fog of meaninglessness which has suffused recent debates.

The peculiarity of the religious situation is that the objects and events referred to in religious beliefs are not directly observable. God, in particular, is said to be wholly unlike or at least to transcend the objects of ordinary experience. It can, therefore, be justly questioned whether the words "wise," "love," "exists," etc., which are applied to God are not so applied with an attendant and entire loss of the content which derives from the ordinary human contexts in which we learn them. What is needed in reply to this question is a positive account of meaning which makes it obvious that no such complete evacuation of empirical meaning is required for sensible discourse about God.

The accounts of religious discourse which first suggest themselves to us are uncongenial: (a) perhaps terms like "wise," are used equivocally when they are applied to God, that is, are used in some

sense completely other than in their creature-des-
ignating uses; or (b) perhaps they are not used in
a different sense but rather in exactly the same way
we use them elsewhere. If (a), then where do the
terms get their new meaning? Are they not empty
of any particular content—with the result that the
religious statements *are* meaningless? If (b), then
the religious utterances must be false because God
is not like the creature and to say God is wise in the
same sense of "wise" we would apply to Socrates
is to say something which even the religious believers would acknowledge to be false. We must look
for a middle ground between the two alternatives.

And is it not obvious that there must be a middle ground? For when we compare two occurrences of a predicate—e.g., "intelligent" in ordinary, nonreligious contexts—"Socrates is intelligent"; "Spaniels are intelligent"—it is almost always
wrong to say the predicate occurs in all its uses with
exactly the same meaning; it is also almost always
wrong to say of any two or more occurrences that
the predicate occurs in completely different and
discontinuous meanings. Wittgenstein[29] (in the
Blue and Brown Books and the *Investigations*) provided overwhelming evidence that ordinary language terms do not have "atoms" of meaning which
are constant, definable, and invariant. He made
it evident that when we compare the meanings of
a term in its various occurrences, the whole set will
with respect to any one of its elements be equivocal,
but not totally equivocal. A family resemblance of
meaning will run throughout the set and will be
recognizable. There must be a middle ground between total equivocation and univocity with respect

[29] Ludwig Wittgenstein, *Philosophical Investigations* (Oxford: Basil Blackwell, 1953); *Blue and Brown Books* (Harper
Torch Book, New York: Harper & Row, 1965).

to two or more occurrences of the same term as a predicate within different sentential contexts. There is, then, a general problem for the philosophy of language: to provide an accurate theoretical account of the similarity of meaning of the occurrences of the same term as it occurs in different contexts. The cases where terms are extended in use to apply to objects which are not directly observable will be merely a subclass of the cases to be accounted for in the general theory.

The theory of analogy (which is the classical answer of the Aristotelian and medieval philosophers to this general problem) was never fully worked out. I will be able to sketch only part of it here. But it is an answer; it does go some of the way toward explaining how cognitive content is preserved in statements which contain terms whose meanings have been extended from contexts which are more directly empirical or observable. The analogy theory is intrinsically interesting and has potentialities which have not been fully appreciated not only for the philosophy of religion, but for the philosophy of language in general.

Since I cannot present a new and general theory of analogy, I shall offer an interpretatively augmented but partial account of the analogy theory employed by St. Thomas Aquinas.

The so-called analogy rules we shall discuss are not thought to be rules one need have in mind while speaking; nor are they thought to be rules with which one merely accords when speaking. Rather, they are rules which are followed, in the same sense in which the basic syntactical regularities and semantical regularities constituting the language are rules which are followed in correct speech. And purported analogy rules are to be subjected to the same empirical establishment or falsification as the other rules of syntax, semantics, and pragmatics. Analogy rules are primarily semantical rules, rules for the attachment of meaning to terms in contexts which are related in an orderly way (a regular way countenanced by the rule for transfer of meaning) to certain basic contexts. Basic contexts will have to be defined alternatively, according to a number of alternative rules for priority of senses of a given term—e.g., we can count "psychologically prior" contexts as basic, or "logically prior" contexts or "chronologically primitive" contexts, or "etymologically prior" contexts as basic. How we select contexts for priority is not important at this point.

In general, let us call something an analogy rule for ordinary language if it is a description of a linguistic regularity whereby a term which occurs in at least two distinct sets of uses (where the distinctness of the sets of uses is established by the fact that the linguistic intention[30] of the term in the one set is not identical with its linguistic intention in the other set) derives its meaning in the one set from its meaning in the other. Specifically, analogy rules will explain the generation of the meanings of some equivocal terms from one another.

There are degrees of equivocation, ranging in principle from zero ("univocity," "identity or one-to-one correspondence of intentions") to complete equivocation, where there is no overlap at all of intentions; so, there may in theory be a large number of kinds of analogy rules and there will probably

---

[30] I mean here by "linguistic intention" of a term "T" the set of all predicates occurring in nonequivalent sentences entailed by a true sentence of the form "x is T." We have a univocal pair of occurrences of "T" when the intentions of "T" in both contexts are in one-to-one correspondence of same trems.

also be pairs of partially equivocal terms whose diverse meanings have no regular or systematic relations within the semantic structure of the language.

For the immediate purposes of the philosophy of religion, there are two well-known analogy rules which St. Thomas and a number of other classical philosophers had observed and which will help explain how we can take terms from empirical contexts and apply them to God. "We cannot speak of God at all except in the language we use of creatures." Naturally, so the terms applied to God will be partially equivocal with respect to their occurrence in ordinary perceptual contexts.

The object of the analogy theory is to explain how it can be that terms like "good," "just" and "cause" do not have exactly the same sense when applied to God that they have when applied to creatures, while arguments from the properties of creatures to the properties of God do not logically equivocate; while we can understand what assertions attributing such predicates to God mean; and while God has nothing precisely in common with any creature. The theory of analogy is designed to permit a middle course between a doctrine which would say that God is so different from His creatures that nothing intelligible can be said of Him in our creature-oriented language, and a doctrine which would say that God is so similar to creatures that no alteration in the meaning of our ordinary predicates is necessary to express truths about His nature and operations. The one view is a complete agnosticism, popular among Neo-platonists and some modern theologians who hold that all religious language is symbolic and must be taken nonliterally. Its assumption of the noncognitivity of religious discourse is, as I have said, false and unjustifiable. The other view is anthropomorphism, which pictures God as merely quantitatively different from objects of experience. The Judaic-Christian religious tradition presupposes a fundamental qualitative and transcendent difference between God and creature, but at the same time assumes that our ordinary language can literally express truths about God, truths which can be accurately conveyed by oral tradition.

The following two passages from St. Thomas Aquinas make clear his understanding of the basic problem and the solution we are advocating; the student should read them carefully. The first is from *Summa Theologica*.[31]

> "I reply that it is impossible that anything should be predicated of both creatures and God univocally. Any effect that falls short of the power of its cause resembles its cause inadequately because it differs from it. Thus, what is found diversely and in various ways in the effect exists simply and in a single way in the cause; so, the sun by a single power produces many different kinds of lower things. In just that way, as we said above (preceeding article), all the perfections which are found among creatures in diverse and various ways preexist in God as united in one.
>
> "When we predicate of creatures some term which indicates a perfection, that term signifies the perfection as something distinct by its definition from every other perfection; for instance, when we predicate the term "wise" of some man, we signify some perfection which is distinct from the essence of the man, and also from his powers and from his existence. But when we predicate such a term of God, we do not intend to signify something which is distinct from His essence, power and existence. Also, when we predicate the term "wise" of some man, it circumscribes and isolates what is signified;

[31] *Summa theologiae* 1.13.5 (tr. J. F. Ross).

but this is not so when the term "wise" is predicated
of God because the reality signified by the term
remains unisolated and exceeds the signification (the
linguistic intention) of the term. Therefore, it is obvious that the term "wise" does not have exactly the
same meaning when predicated of God and of some
creature. And the same reasoning holds for all the
other terms which indicate perfection. So no term
is predicated of God and creatures univocally.

"But the terms are not used purely equivocally,
either, as some have claimed. For, if that were so,
nothing would be knowable or demonstrable concerning God from our knowledge of creatures; our
reasoning would always commit the fallacy of equivocation. Such a view would be as discordant with
the philosophers who demonstrate a number of
things about God, as it would be with the Apostle
Paul who said: "The invisible things of God are
made known by the things that are made."

"We have to say, then, that terms are used of
creatures and God analogously, that is, according
to an ordering between them. We can distinguish
two ways in which analogy based upon the order
among things can be found among terms: First one
word may be used of two things because each of
them has some order or relation to a third thing.
Thus we use the term "healthy" of both medicine
and urine because both things have a relation to
another thing, namely the health of the animal, of
which the latter is the sign and the former the cause.
Secondly, one word may be used of two things
because of the relation the one thing has to the
other; thus "healthy" is used of both the medicine
and the animal because the medicine is the cause
of the health in the man. In this way some terms
are used of creatures and God, neither univocally
nor purely equivocally, but analogously.

"We are unable to speak of God except in the
language we use of creatures, as we said above
(1.13.1). And so, whatever is said of both creatures
and God is said on the basis of the order or relation

which holds between the creature and God, namely, that God is the source and cause in which all the perfections of things preexist eminently.

"This kind of community is a middle-ground between pure equivocation and simple univocity. For among those terms which are used analogously, there is not a common or single concept, as there is among univocal terms; but neither are the concepts wholly diverse, as is the case among equivocal terms. Rather, the term which is predicated in different ways signifies different relations to some one thing; thus "healthy" when predicated of urine means "is a sign of the health of the animal", whereas when predicated of the medicine it means "is a cause of the health of the animal".

The second passage from St. Thomas Aquinas is from his *Disputed Questions: On Truth*.[32]

"Nothing can be predicated of a creature and of God univocally. For when a term is used univocally of more than one thing, what the term signifies is common to each of the things of which it is univocally predicated. So far as the signification of the term is concerned, the things of which it is univocally predicated are undifferentiated, even though they may precede one another in being; for instance, all numbers are equally numbers although one is prior to another. But no matter how much a creature may resemble God, a point cannot be reached at which something belongs to it and to God for the same reason. For things which are in different subjects and have the same formal definition are common to the subjects in substance and quiddity but are distinct in *esse*. Whatever is in God, however, is His own *esse*; for just as His essence is the same as His *esse*, so His knowledge is the same as His knowing. Since the *esse* which is proper to one thing cannot be communicated to another, it cannot happen that a creature should ever attain to having something for the same reason that God has it be-

[32] 2.11 (translated by J. F. Ross).

cause it is impossible that the creature should come into possession of the same *esse* as is God's. The same is true for us; if 'man' and 'to *be* as a man' did not differ in Peter and Paul, it would not be possible for the term "man" to be predicated univocally of Peter and of Paul whose *esse* is distinct.

"Still, it cannot be maintained that whatever is predicated of God and a creature is predicated purely equivocally because if there were not some real resemblance between the creature and God, His essence would not be a likeness of creatures, and thus He could not understand creatures by understanding His essence. Similarly, we would not be able to come to know God from created things either; nor would it be that from among the terms which apply to creatures, one rather than another, ought to be predicated of God; for with equivocal terms it makes no difference which is applied since the term does not imply any real agreement among the things to which it applies.

"So we have to say that the term "knowledge" is predicated of God's knowledge and of ours neither wholly univocally nor purely equivocally. Instead it is predicated analogously, which is the same as proportionally.

"Resemblance on account of a proportion (relation) can be of two kinds, and so two kinds of analogous community can be distinguished. There is a community between things of which one is related to another in virtue of their having a fixed distance or other determinate relationship to each other, as the number 2 to the number 1, in that the former is the double of the latter. Sometimes there is a community (or resemblance) between two things, not accounted for because the one is a function of the other but rather, because of a likeness of two relations; for instance, 6 resembles 4 in that as 6 is the double of 3, so is 4 the double of 2. The first kind of resemblance is one of proportion; the second is one of parity of proportion or proportionality.

"We find something said analogically of two

things in virtue of the first type of resemblance when one of them has a direct and determinate relationship to the other, as, for instance, "being" is predicated of accident and of substance because of the relationship which accident has to substance; and "healthy" is predicated of urine and of an animal because urine has some relation to the health of the animal. Sometimes something is predicated analogically in virtue of the second type of resemblance, as when the term "sight" is predicated of bodily sight and of the understanding, because sight is to the eye what understanding is to the mind.

"There must be some determinate (definite) relationship between things to which something is common by analogy of the first sort; consequently, it cannot be that anything is predicated of God and creatures by this type of analogy because no creature has such a determinate relationship to God. But the other type of analogy requires no determinate type of relationship between the things in which something is common by analogy; and so nothing excludes some term's being predicated analogously of God and creatures in this manner.

"This can happen in two ways: sometimes the term implies that something, which cannot be common to God and a creature even in a proportionality, belongs to what it primarily designated. This is so of everything which is predicated metaphorically of God, as when He is said to be a lion, the sun, and so forth, because the definitions include matter which cannot be attributed to God. In other cases, a term which is used of God and creatures has no implications in its primary uses which preclude a resemblance of the kind described between God and creatures. To this class belong all those predicates which do not imply a defect (limitation) and which do not depend upon matter for their *esse*; for instance, "being", "good" and so forth."

The religious utterances which are characteristic of the Christian's expression of faith are not in a technical language and do not employ a scientific vocabulary. Rather, such utterances as "God is almighty," "God loves the world," "God created the heavens and the earth," "God is good," are as much part of ordinary language as are utterances concerning the weather, domestic or business affairs and community relationships. Theological statements about God in a scientifically refined systematic discourse are derived in meaningfulness from ordinary discourse; theological statements are theoretical. Hence the extended or restricted meaning of those predicates of religious claims which occur in ordinary discourse must first be explained. Then the theoretically developed language of theology and philosophy can perhaps be justified.

Analogy Rules

Let us call statements which attribute some predicate P to God, "G-statements" and statements which attribute some predicate P to creatures, "E-statements" (that is, statements about objects of natural experience). Wherever a predicate P occurs in a logically consistent, affirmative G-statement, it is not univocal with (does not have exactly the same meaning as) P when it occurs in an E-statement which is both affirmative and logically consistent. Thus, sentence (1) "Socrates is good," employs "good" in a sense different from its sense in (2) "God is good." But the uses are not totally equivocal. (Otherwise the meanings of the terms applied to God would have to be learned nonempirically, something which is admitted by all parties to the dispute not to have happened.)

What is signified by P in (1) is the same as what is signified by P in (2). But the mode of signification is different since the mode of signification depends upon the mode of being by which the subject possesses or could possess the predicate. For instance, God is by nature or "essentially" good. The creature is contingently good, dependently good. Secondly, God's existence is independent and necessary; the creature's existence is dependent and contingent. Hence, the mode of being appropriate to each is different. This affects the sense (the intention) of the predicate in a way that cannot be spelled out.

Let us see why this difference in intention cannot be spelled out. The divergence of sense between P in (1) and P in (2) cannot be eliminated by the construction of any new predicate Q, which is supposed to capture the meaning of P as it applies exclusively to God, since the only way we can understand what saying "God is Q" means would be by first understanding what it would mean to say of some creature, "x is Q"; but since Q by supposition is a predicate not applicable to creatures (because it was designed to express the mode of being proper to God), it follows that we could not understand the assertion "x is Q." Hence the analogical predicate cannot be eliminated in favor of a univocal predicate applicable to both things and God.[33] This is why many theologians have insisted that analogy is the *form* of human speech about God, and that the analogous predicates cannot be eliminated or reductively replaced without the abandonment of all sense for our God-statements.

A careful reading of Wittgenstein will, I think,

---

[33] Of course, we can design a *disjunctive* predicate which will apply to God and creatures univocally, but it will be an artificial predicate derived from the analogous pair and will lack any explanatory value. We could make up "wise 1 or wise 2" where "wise 1" means "wise as in sentence (1)" and "wise 2" means "wise as in sentence (2)." Both God and Socrates will then bear that constructed predicate. It will be univocal but composed of analogous parts. There are a number of other problems connected with this; but we shall have to by-pass them now.

disclose an even broader conclusion: that analogy is part of the structure of ordinary discourse in general; that the systematically related meanings of terms like "knows," "believes," "wants," "chooses," in their various uses cannot be reductively eliminated through general definitions.

Now consider what it means to say that a predicate is analogous. A predicate cannot be analogous by itself. Rather, it is analogous in one use with respect to another use or class of uses (in statements). So too, by the way, with "univocal," "equivocal," "synonymous," etc.—all these predicates presuppose a number of occurrences of the terms which are to bear them[34] and presuppose that factors other than the terms themselves determine which of those predicates are appropriate. Thus the term "good" is analogous in its G-statement uses with respect to its E-statement uses; that is, "good" in the G-statements is dependent upon and derived in meaning from "good" in its E-statement occurrences (where the E-statements are affirmative and logically consistent). Scholastics generally adopted two different sets of conditions which are sufficient for its being the case that a predicate has been used analogously with respect to its several uses. The sets of conditions relate different usages of the same term in ordinary language and are thus said to preserve the meaningfulness of the term when religious discourse conforms to those rules, simply because it is obvious that the ordinary language changes in the sense of predicates according to these rules preserve meaningfulness for the derived assertions in nonreligious contexts.

[34] However, it may be all right to define a reflexive sense of those terms such that (a) every term is univocal with itself in numerically the same occurrence; (b) every term is synonymous with itself in numerically the same occurrence; (c) no term is ever equivocal with itself or analogous with itself in numerically the same occurrence; etc.

The first rule is called the *analogy of attribution*. It states that the same term "t" can occur as predicate in two different statements, e.g., (A) "Fido is healthy," and (B) "Fido's complexion is healthy," where the subject of the one statement actually possesses the property of health, while the subject of the other (B) is merely a cause, a sign, or a condition for the subject of (A)'s having that property, and in fact could not possess the property possessed by the subject of (A). In (B) the predicate "t" is attributed to a subject which does not possess it (i.e., the complexion has health attributed to it but is not itself the subject of health), on account of that subject's relationship to what does possess it, the dog. The predicate healthy in the two cases is equivocal, but not entirely so; rather the entire definition of "t" in (A) is part of the definition of "t" in (B). There are other conditions for this kind of analogy too, notably conditions of priority of predication; but this will do as a sketch.

Thus is will be seen that some things will be predicated of God—for example, being our life—which God does not possess formally, but only possesses by attribution; possesses on account of His causal or conserving relationship to our experiencing certain effects. Some philosophers have thought that attribution is the most fundamental form of analogy, but these thinkers are in the minority and are surely in error. The analogy of attribution has many important functions but it is not fundamental to the theory of religious language; not all predicates in assertions about God are used by analogy of attribution with respect to other basic ordinary language uses of those same terms. Many things are attributed to God which God possesses both formally and essentially—for example: intelligence, existence, power, love. It is impossible that God should have all His attributes in relation to (as cause, sign of, etc.) the attributes of finite things. This is inconsistent with the divine independence and priority in being. Those terms which name the other divine attributes must derive their meanings from empirical predicates in another way.

The second analogy rule, called the *analogy of proper proportionality*, is generally considered to be the basis of the meaningfulness of religious language. It is assumed by the conditions for this sort of analogy that there are similarities between God's relationships to His actual and possible operations and man's (or some other creature's) relationship to his actual or possible operations. Thus if "Socrates is good" is true, Socrates stands dispositionally in a relationship to some activity or acts of his in a way similar to that in which God stands to His being or acts when it is true that God is good. The term "good" is employed in speaking of God just because we recognize the similarity of His relationship to the relationship we call "being good" with respect to a creature. So also with all other terms applied to God. The reason why the term is not univocal in these divergent uses is that there is an essential difference between the beings, a difference in mode of being. Thus it is correct to say "Fido knows his master" and "Socrates knows his teacher." But the term "knows," while expressing a *similar* relationship, does not express the same relationship since the mode of knowledge possessed by Socrates is different from that possessed by Fido. This example is given to suggest, without the elaboration necessary for a full explanation, how the same sort of shift in sense which is held to characterize religious discourse also occurs in other areas of ordinary language and follows the same rule. Perhaps the most striking example of such a shift in sense is in the statements: "Hamlet exists," "Socrates exists," and "The number 1 exists." In these three statements the term "exists" differs in meaning depending upon the mode of being properly attributable to each one of the subjects; Hamlet does not exist as numbers do, and numbers do not inhabit space and time.

Between the world described in E-statements—the world of sensible experience—and some entity not part of the world (God), there obtain certain relations—e.g., "being moved by"; "being efficiently caused by"; "being conserved in existence by"; "being excelled by"; "being designed by." (These relations correspond to concepts employed in the five existential arguments of St. Thomas, and are mentioned because of their classical status, not because I consider them fundamental or privileged.)

A term which signifies these relations—let us take only one for consideration, say "being caused by"—cannot be used in exactly the same way as it is used in a sentence like this: "My black eye was caused by John." For this is an E-statement, and the fundamental assumption is that God will not have any properties or relations in the same way as any of His creatures, since God's being is self-explanatory and the creature's is not.

So, the argument is: God is at most proportionally similar to John (that is, is not directly similar but stands in a similar relation) because the relation "being caused by" is similar (but not identical) in the statements of the form (A) WCg (The world is caused by God) and (B) BCj (The black eye is caused by John). And the term "being caused by" is analogous by proportionality. "Being caused by" has the same signification in both cases, but differs in intention because of the different modes of being connoted in the two cases. The reason why we cannot replace this term ("being caused by") with a univocal term is that in (A) the mode of signification which is proper to "C" in (B) has been cancelled out in the context (A). We do not know the distinguishing characteristics of the mode of possession by which God has His properties: so, we cannot fill in the part of the signification which is cancelled out. Thus the term "being caused by," while having all elements of its meaning present which are necessary to distinguish "being caused by" from any other relation, still does not have present the elements by which to distinguish the divine mode of being from the finite mode. And yet, even if these latter modal elements were present, the term would still be equivocal because the modal elements of "C" in (A) and "C" in (B) would be different. We say therefore that the *signification* of "C" is the same in both sentences but the intentions of "C" differ partially from one another.

All natural knowledge of God consists basically in finding that certain relationships within possible worlds actually obtain between things that exist and God.

These relation terms, which are analogous by proper proportionality with instances of the same terms in statements about the world, are then transferred into names or predicates of the other relatum, God. This transference of relation terms into names follows the rule of analogy of attribution. You can call a person by the names of his characteristic activities because he is dispositionally the cause of his actions which, in turn, reveal and constitute his activities. Thus, we call a man who smokes a smoker and a man who judges a judge, and a man who designs, a designer. And transforming the name of an effect into a name of the cause is an instance of analogy of attribution. So, the entity X which has the relation "being the remote or immediate cause of all other entities and events" is called "First Cause."

Next, utilizing the fact that secondary employments of terms analogous by attribution still tell us something about the subject, St. Thomas and the neoscholastic writers generally proceed to decide what properties God would have to have if He is the cause, the judge, the conserver, etc. And thus, they arrive at the properties of intelligence, free will, simplicity, etc. But these terms can all be regarded as relational predicates and can be shown to be analogous by proportionality ("similarity of relations") with respect to ordinary language occurrences of the same terms—occurrences which are psychologically and epistemically prior.

Hence, all statements about God employ terms which are analogous by proper proportionality with respect to psychologically prior occurrences of the same terms in statements describing ordinary experience. Analogy of proper proportionality is therefore, the general form of language about God.

Thus, there are two basic kinds of statements made in discussing the existence and nature of God: (A) statements that some relation R obtains between entities of a certain kind (the things of the world) and some entity not a member of that kind, God; and (B) statements which employ cognate forms of the relation-term "R" as common nouns or adjectives either to name or to describe the entity. An example of (A) is "everything which has really distinct properties is causally dependent upon some entity which does not have really distinct properties; and, there are some entities which have distinct properties." An example of (B) is "there exists a First Cause." It is immediately obvious that statements of set (B) logically presuppose both the truth and meaningfulness of statements of set (A). How set (B) is derived from (A) was described above. The relation terms that occur in sentences of set (A) are said to be analogous by proper proportionality with ordinary language occurrences of the same terms.

Another point: A term can occur as predicate in a negative G-statement and be used univocally with its occurrence in an affirmative E-statement. Thus, "God is not corporeal" and "Animals are corporeal." A term can also be used as a predicate in an affirmative G-statement and still be used univocally with its occurrence in an affirmative E-statement (which is consistent), but with the result that the G-statement is necessarily false. For instance, "God is wise" where "wise" is univocal with "wise" in "Socrates is wise." Conformity to the analogy rules is a prerequisite for consistency in statements about God. If the predicates do not undergo changes of meaning which bring their connotations into conformity with the mode of being of the subject, the statement will be logically absurd and necessarily false. The structure of ordinary language is rigid enough to require us to indicate explicitly that in certain cases we are using terms univocally of God, as in the example above.

Some statements about God employ terms which, besides being used analogously by proportionality with respect to E-statements, are also used analogously by attribution with respect to other and logically prior G-statements. That is, the statement "the actual world is caused by God" is logically prior to "God is the First Cause." The statements which attribute common names to God employ predicates analogous by attribution with respect to instances of the same predicates occurring in statements asserting that certain relations obtain between the world and God. Thus, to say "God is the artificer, the designer, the judge," etc., is to employ as a common name a term which by both logical and psychological priority is employed in a statement that "the world is made, planned, and judged by God."

In broad outline this is the structure of the analogy theory. To succeed as an account of religious discourse, it is essential that analogy (systematic derivation of meaning among equivocal terms) be shown to be a general feature of ordinary language; the forms of the systematic derivations of meaning be described in clearly stated "analogy rules"; the fundamental elements of religious discourse (i.e., the predicates to be attributed to God) be shown to be related to their occurrences in E-statements in ways which the analogy rules for ordinary language will actually explain. While the details of a general theory of analogy have never been worked out for ordinary language as a whole, enough explanatory power is observable in the rules for "analogy of attribution" and "analogy of proper proportionality" to suggest that an account of religious discourse as essentially analogical while cognitively meaningful is practicable and likely to be convincing.

In this chapter, I have tried to explain why the noncognitivist approaches to religious discourse are inherently implausible and, by an interpreted outline of St. Thomas' analogy theory, that a cognitivist account of religious discourse holds great promise despite its incompleteness.

The problems of the philosophy of religion are, in general, not problems peculiar to the subject matter of religion. The reason we don't have a satisfactory account of the cognitivity of religious discourse is primarily that we don't have an adequate account of meaning derivation in general, despite the wonderful liveliness with which Wittgenstein shows us the problem again and again. Perhaps our time will see the solution of these problems since we have been so vastly helped by the observation of Aquinas and Wittgenstein.

CONCLUSION

In each of the four chapters I have tried to show you certain representative and traditional opinions on the questions treated, (a) the establishment of the existence of God, (b) nontheoretical knowledge of God through faith and experience, (c) the problem of evil, (d) the analogy theory of religious language. I have also illustrated certain advances which are characteristic of contemporary analytic philosophy in the hope that you will pursue these matters and will consult the recent literature noted in the bibliography and chosen sparingly so that it will not overwhelm you.

You might wonder (after consulting some general introduction to the philosophy of religion) why we chose to discuss the epistemological problem of knowing God through faith and experience rather than to delve in detail into the extensive twentieth century debate over the meaningfulness of religious discourse and its relation to empirical verification and falsification. The answer is that in my opinion the beneficial results of that debate have been too largely negative. General study by philosophers of language has eventuated in almost universal rejection of "verifiability" or "falsifiability" as a decisive criterion of meaningfulness; the examination of whether religious language is primarily cognitive or noncognitive has revealed only confusion over the distinction; and the verification theory of meaning has been found, in the case of religious discourse, to have simply begged the question of whether believers are in a position to know which religious claims are true and which are false. Hence, it seems that a new approach to the problem of religious discourse must be undertaken by way of a more careful application of the theory of knowledge to the beliefs of religious persons. It is the introduction to this enterprise which we have substituted in Chapter II. A student who wishes to go further in his study of the philosophy of religion should certainly pursue the development of the verification controversy and should also go much more deeply into the questions of divine foreknowledge, omniscience, predestination, grace, immortality, and personal identity. Knowing the history of these discussions is vital because it makes intelligible the structure of present-day disputes and saves the student from a useless repetition of old errors.

Above all else, I hope to have convinced the student that a painstaking analytical reconsideration of traditional questions about religion is philosophically satisfying and productive; that contemporary philosophy has much to offer our understanding of religion; and that religion and theology can be and should be the subject matter for precise, dispassionate and rational discourse.

Selected Bibliography

Text Anthologies (which contain the main classical statements on the important problems, as well as significant recent statements).

1. *Philosophy of Religion: A Book of Reading,* George L. Abernethy and Thomas A. Langford (New York, The Macmillan Company, second edition, 1968).
2. *Classical and Contemporary Readings in the Philosphy of Religion,* John Hick (Englewood Cliffs, N.J., Prentice Hall, 1963).
3. *Readings in Religious Philosophy,* McGregor and Robb (Boston, Houghton-Mifflin Co., 1962). This anthology gives special attention to the recent discussion of religious discourse.
4. *Readings in the Philosophy of Religion,* John A. Mourant (New York, Thomas Y. Crowell Company, 1962). (Good selections on faith, predestination and immortality.)

Collections of Essays

1. *New Essays in Philosophical Theology,* A. Flew and A. MacIntyre, ed. (New York, The Macmillan Company, 1955). In paperback now.
2. *Faith and Logic,* Basil Mitchell, ed. (London, George Allen and Unwin, Ltd., 1957).

3. *God and Evil,* Nelson Pike, ed. (Englewood Cliffs, N.J., Prentice-Hall, 1964).

Special Works

1. *A Proof of God's Existence: Recent Essays on the Ontological Argument,* Hick and McGill, eds. (New York, The Macmillan Company, 1965).
2. *The Logic of Perfection,* Charles Hartshorne (Lasalle, Illinois, Open Court Publishing Co., 1962).
3. *Aquinas,* Frederic Copleston (London, Penguin Books, 1955).
4. *The Universe—Plan or Accident,* R.E.D. Clark (Philadelphia, Muhlenburg Press, 1961).
5. *Faith and Knowledge,* John Hick (Ithaca, New York, Cornell University Press, 1957).
6. *Our Experience of God,* H.D. Lewis (New York, The Macmillan Company, 1959).
7. *Love Almighty and Ills Unlimited,* Austin Farrer (New York, Doubleday and Company, Inc., 1961).
8. *Language, Logic and God,* Frederick Ferré (New York, Harper & Row, 1961).
9. *Studies in Christian Existentialism,* J. Macquarrie (London, SCM Press, 1966).

INDEX

Index